AMONG
ISLANDS

By the same author:

*St Kilda**
The Royal Mile
*West Highland Landscape**
*Glencoe – Monarch of Glens**
A High and Lonely Place
Discovering the Pentland Hills
Waters of the Wild Swan
*Shetland – Land of the Ocean**
Among Mountains

*With photographer Colin Baxter

AMONG ISLANDS

JIM CRUMLEY

MAINSTREAM
PUBLISHING

EDINBURGH AND LONDON

First published in Great Britain in 1994 by
MAINSTREAM PUBLISHING COMPANY
(EDINBURGH) LTD
7 Albany Street
Edinburgh EH1 3UG

ISBN 1 85158 619 9

The publisher gratefully acknowledges the financial
assistance of The Scottish Arts Council in the production
of this book.

A catalogue record for this book is available from the
British Library

Phototypeset in Sabon by Intype, London
Printed in Spain by AGT
D.L.TO:930-1994

To George Mackay Brown

ACKNOWLEDGMENTS

The author would like to thank the following for assisting the cause of this book: George Garson, Andy Currie, David Craig, Marion Campbell, Colin Baxter. This is a good place, too, to acknowledge how much the writing of George Mackay Brown has meant to me over the years. No island voice sings clearer than his.

CONTENTS

Puffin and kittiwake on a stubborn shore: characteristic ingredients of island-ness

Chapter One

ISLAND-NESS

'IS THIS THE last boat?' I asked the Yell ferryman, for the advertised schedule appeared to have acquired an unfathomable flexibility during the day.

'No . . . no . . .' he replied, his face as becalmed and unsmiling as Yell Sound, 'there will be boats again all day tomorrow.'

He held my eye and I held his and it was gray, quite gray, and tranquil as slack water. But then a tern flicked past, laughing, and that was humour enough for the three of us (the islander, the mainlander, the globetrotter) so that when our eyes met again, we were all laughing.

I love Yell. It is low and blunt and self-contained, and its every distant view reveals not just its island nature, but also that it is an island among islands, a still centre around which the rest of Shetland whirls its wind-dervishes. I love islands, some more than others, because what I love most is island-ness and that phenomenon is unequally distributed among islands.

Island-ness? I have always struggled for a compact definition, which is careless because it is my own word. But the way the sea lies in the sound between island and mainland (or between islands) that is different from the way the sea dives into the same island's ocean-going shores . . . that is island-ness. There again, the way a high moor dips to the head of sea loch, voe or inlet and a seal crops up more moorland than ocean . . . that, too, is island-ness. The way you climb to the summit of a small hill and turn through 360 degrees and see no land other than the worn-down mountain stub on which you stand . . . that is island-ness. So is the way a passing tern creases a ferryman's poker face.

The diminishing, paling profile of St Kilda from the capricious deck of a two-masted Mull-bound schooner, diminishing and paling and smudging and crumpling over hours until it levels and sinks and is gone from the sea . . . that is island-ness. And when you tie up in Tobermory at 7 a.m. on a flat and golden and already hot June morning and you have been up since 4 a.m., roused by the mate to watch a killer whale cross your bows at a hundred yards and the Skye Cuillin slip by incomprehensibly, miles to the east (those same Cuillin which stand among the westmost mountains of my mind) . . . that is the kind of island-ness which can mark a mainlander for life and colour all his days so that somewhere deep within him he yearns forever for an encircling sea. In the June of 1988 I made such a voyage, tasted such an island-ness, and whenever I can put my face to a sea wind and close my eyes, the taste of it is in the back of my throat again, pungent and undiminished.

There is yet another species of island-ness. It is the one which pervades as an irrepressible spirit the decks of a ferryboat. The *St Ola*, for example, has sailed in several manifestations between Scotland and Orkney since 1892. The brunt of all that seafaring and Pentland Firthing was borne by the first *Ola*. One who knew her all too well is my great friend George Garson who wears his Orcadian lineage with a quiet pride. In his stylish wee book *Orkney All the Way Through*, he writes of that old wave-butter thus:

> She was black, blunt-stemmed, narrow-gutted, coal-fired and reeked of stale vomit and fear-filled cattle. But I know old Stromnessians who boast still of her legendary sea-worthiness; of how, with cocky panache, she plied continuously that fickle stretch of water from 1892 to 1951. I feared and hated her!

Today's *Ola* has pink carpets and video games and stabilizers and her cargo is often as much tourist as islander, but she wears her island-ness with the same fervour that she did when tourists to Orkney were hardy pipe-smoking professors in tweed jackets and thick coats pursuing an academic species of birdwatching which is now all but extinct. The *Ola* may have evolved a state-of-the-art indifference to storms and tides, computerised and plasticated to an extent which would have had any nineteenth-century shipwright worth his salt spluttering in his ale, but she is nevertheless still a floating fragment of Orkney imbued with a presence, an island-ness, which stems directly from her lineage. Orkney is why she exists, and when she ties up alongside Stromness on a Saturday night the islands are intact again, their prodigal firth-plier home again, until Monday at least, and Orkney is smoored in its own calm afterglow of self-containment. That, too, is island-ness and you can recognise its like on every vessel anywhere which is yoked to an island crossing. It is why people still sing 'The Skye Boat Song' to themselves when they cross from Kyle of Lochalsh: they taste Skye on the ferry, and they will never taste it on a bridge. It cuts no ice with governments and public inquiries, but one of the most compelling arguments I know against a bridge to Skye is the damage it will inflict on Skye's island-ness. The day the bridge opens and Skye becomes not an island but a peninsula is the day that it loses that crucial self-containment the Orcadian knows, crucial to the psychological wellbeing of all islanders.

Thirty-five years ago I stood on the slipway at Kyle of Lochalsh at the centre of a family argument. We were four – my parents, my older brother and I – and the argument was about going over on the ferry and back just so that we could say we had set foot on Skye. My mother and brother were all for going, but the idea stuck in my craw, irretrievably lodged there by half-baked instincts, reasons I could not possibly articulate at the time, and I protested. I had no way of knowing how much Skye in particular and islands in general would colour my later life, yet I was angry with an uncomprehending certainty that merely alighting on Skye like a bee on a flower, pollinating tourism as it were, was no way to greet so famous an island. How could I, a 12-year-old east-coast mainlander, have acquired even the flimsiest sense of the sensibilities of islands? Yet even from this distance and with more than twenty-five years of island-lingering to rum-mage through for reference points, the recalled fervour of my protest still surprises and baffles me. My father, for reasons of his own which I did not understand then and understand even less even now, threw me his all-powerful support and we drove north for Sutherland. It is too late now to ask him why.

The episode served only to push the *idea* of islands a little more forcefully towards the front of a mind already eagerly receptive to nature and the wilder faces of the Scottish landscape. The following year we moved from our beloved prefab to the newly built top-floor flat of a four-storey block high on the slopes of the Balgay Hill, one of the two centrepiece hills which characterise the unkindly unsung landscape of my native Dundee. From that unlikeliest of settings I made my first wildly speculative discoveries about the nature of islands. We were all reluctant flat-dwellers after the farmland freedoms of the prefab years, but that flat's saving graces were the hill at its back and a miles-wide view of the Tay estuary which was the envy of every visitor who happened to chance on the right kind of day or night. The right kind of day was one on which the Tay's seagoing horizon was a hard blue line, broken only by a single white and far-off smudge. It was visible only on the clearest days (most often in the earliest of paper-round mornings) but even on the grayest of days, shrouded in fog or storm, you knew it was there and you never ceased to marvel at what it stood for. On

*Yell Sound: tern-haunted thoroughfare to the island at the still
centre of Shetland*

The hills of Hoy on a quiet Sunday when 'Orkney is smoored in its own calm afterglow of self-containment'

Isle Ornsay: 'merely alighting on Skye like a bee on a flower, polinating tourism as it were, was no way to greet so famous an island . . .'

the frost-black nights or through pale-skied dusks and fiery dawns, it shone at you down the sea miles, a flickering glimmer which whispered of other worlds, the Bell Rock lighthouse.

It stood (it still does) twenty-something miles off my native Angus shore on a rock of incomprehensible loneliness and it made a turbulent impression on my teenage years, infiltrating dreams and daydreams. It was in its time populated by a curious and intriguing species of incarcerated seamen, the most unimaginably land-locked existence with only the sea-fear, the sea-splendour, the sea-power for company. It is long since automated of course, which seems a pity only if you dreamed my kind of dreams or if you were hewn from that remarkable tribe of lighthousekeepers, rock-like themselves in their stoicism. The best of it must have been a kind of blissful mesmerism, friend to bird and mariner and whale. The worst of it was the vilest of hells, wrestling with the relentless weeks of storm for a hold on your sanity, craving in winter darkness the short feeble gray winter daylight, beyond rescue, praying for calms. All the Bell Rock's shades coloured my young dreams, and long before I set foot on my first island (Skye inevitably), I had gleaned something of what it takes to be an islander, something of that mixed blessing of island-ness which swithers perpetually somewhere between the Bell Rock's extremes of isolation and the warm stuff-the-world security of the raised drawbridge.

Quietly we went down
down to the shore and stood,
while blackly the boats
went by to their war
and were merely beautiful
in their orderly going.

Someone called for three cheers
for King and wave-ruling country
but none was raised above
the quiet of our shore-going.
It was not (another said)
our navy nor our war –
and besides – the island
had given too much
to soldiery as it was.

Quietly we went up
up from the shore and closed
one by one the island doors,
while blackly the boats
withdrew their beautiful shadows
from our waters.

Dundee accommodated another symbol of islands, one which vexed my imagination more than even the Bell Rock's faery-flicker. It hung incongruously, monstrously, from the room of the city museum; it looked as if someone, perhaps a caveman, had designed the prototype frame for the first airship, and using such materials as he had to hand, had made it out of bits of bone. It was the skeleton of the Tay whale, and who thought it should be best viewed from fifty feet below is one of those mysteries which were built into the fabric of museums of a certain age. There it flew, a skeletal whale, and there it insinuated its way into the nightmares of untold generations of Dundee children. It has since flitted (no meagre achievement in a dead leviathan) along the street to a slightly better viewing arrangement, but it haunts still. A whale needs an ocean's context in which to be understood, but what I have always understood from that wretched creature which ended its days high and dry and unharpooned on a Tay sandbank was that the thousands of men who steamed north from Dundee over a couple of centuries to wrest such creatures from their comprehending ocean were either inhuman or superhuman or most likely both. Dundee's was the biggest whaling fleet in Britain, a city on the lips of the world's mariners, and when its ships sailed for the whaling grounds of the North Atlantic they put in first at Stromness in Orkney, or Lerwick in Shetland, for water, supplies, men. What they have left in their wake is an association of waterfronts, mainlander and islander, a mingled lineage, a seafarer's bond, and an ear on which the hard-edged, wide-vowelled speech of the other falls kindly. So it is not hard for an east-coast mainlander to go among the islands and the islanders of the north, feel the kin of their island-ness.

So that, as far as I am concerned, was the psychological implant which set the tiller of my instincts rummaging among islands. But I came late to the Northern Isles, early to the West, and for that there is a more prosaic reason. It is tempting to dwell on the fruits of a perfunctory research by a great-uncle who found my family's origins in seventeenth-century Ireland (Waterford cattle rustlers he insisted, without revealing his sources and I was too young at the time to have the nerve to ask for them). With Celtic brigands for ancestors – why shouldn't I stand on the brim of the Minch with a Columba-was-here lump in my throat? Reality, alas, is that I

Old Orkney farmstead: 'It is not hard for an east coast mainlander to go easily among the islands and the islanders of the north, feel the kin of their island-ness . . .'

Hoy, Orkney: 'I have lingered where memories are fondest and impressions deepest, or where I am most eager for return . . .'

wandered west in pursuit of its mountains, and if anything as heart-stopping as the Cuillin afloat in their ocean might be deemed prosaic, I came to Skye for the Cuillin. But I stayed, and I have returned two or three or more times almost every one of the intervening twenty-five years for Skye's island-ness, of which the Cuillin are simply a monumental component. But Skye, too, is an island among islands, and once you have sipped the addiction of crossing straits and sounds, you start to eye the bits of ocean to windward with their unfamiliar island shapes. The high ground of Skye is washed by an Eden of temptations for the island-addicted. Over the years I have succumbed to almost all of them, and found no dull shore in the seas of the Hebrides.

This is my fourth book about islands. The first was my first book, about St Kilda, the second was Shetland, the third Skye. This one alights on these and other shores, tying the threads of journeys and years and motives together, a single notional voyage among the islands of my life. In its companion volume, *Among Mountains*, I wrote: 'In sifting this book from my own mountain years, I have purposely dwelled on those mountains which have made impressions on my life I will never shake off . . . ' I have likewise lingered here where memories are fondest and impressions deepest, or where I am most eager for return. It is, in truth, the book about the addiction, and that too is island-ness.

Chapter Two

A LONG WAIT IN THE WIND

THEY DON'T SAY 'tern' on Yell, they say 'tirrick', or at least the old folk do. It is a good name, appropriately percussive for (on Yell or anywhere else) it is what the arctic tern says: '*Tirrick*!', and like most 'ick' sounds which roll of the tongue of any Shetlander it emerges as 'eek'. And it holds a faintly hysterical edge to it, ripping out of a slender serenity into a fine red rage at the least provocation, so the arctic tern, when it is not impersonating Shetlanders, is impersonating Shetland's weather.

April is a poor thing in Shetland, gray-faced and hollow-cheeked, withered by winter. One April stirs in the memory more than others. The winter which preceded it was a gale, all of it, one gale which scarcely paused to gather breath. The snow, when it bothered to fossilise the rain at all, never lingered. There would be one blinding-bright morning, a tinselly handful of hours might tremble in the islanders' unaccustomed eyes. Then the wind would be all skinny ragged-edged knives, but inevitably the gray blind (the Shetlander's more accustomed winter shade) would fall again and the wind would be all fat and slobbering bullies. So by April, when sooth-moothers contemplate a new season fat-budded and greening, Yell lies low and gray and comatose and still. Kensington Gardens, London, meanwhile, was shirt-sleeved, flower-bright and warm. I had a morning-after stroll there consoling myself after the futile pursuit of a publisher, a literary project mercifully stillborn (we all have them, some more than others). At the same time, though, it seemed like a mortal blow to my writer's aspirations, and as I strolled among birdsong and Browning-esque England I told myself it was undeniably beautiful, seductive too, then I caught myself wondering traitorous thoughts about life in London if I really wanted to write for a living. Then, this happened:

'They don't say "tern" on Yell, they say "trirrick" . . .'

In the late morning, I flew to Edinburgh. Through the afternoon I drove flat out for Aberdeen and by something like half past three I was in the P&O carpark glowering morosely up at decapitated container trucks (for this carpark is where juggernauts go to die) and cattle floats which steamed and bellowed and stank, and other unfathomable diesel-powered monsters. By dawn I was sailing past Sumburgh, well-slept and showered, swithering between starboard for the sunrise show on the sea and port for its glow on Sumburgh's kittiwake cliffs; by nine I was hot breakfasting in Lerwick and by noon I was face-to-pasty-face with Yell, Yell as bemused and becalmed as a beached whale and suspended now in a state of spring-less April torpor. A mile from the ferry I stopped the car, stopped moving, stepped out into the island's wan welcome, scented the island-ness of where I stood (a peat-and-salt-air concoction that never fails), and recognised at once in the landscape what was missing in Kensington, what for me would always be missing in Kensington: a kinship with a sense of place.

You could never argue with any conviction that Yell is a beautiful place, not beautiful at least in the sense of Foula's fabulous little crop of hills or Nibon's sea valley or Weisdale's long and island-spattered voe. Yell is too low to the ground for all that, its one hilltop no more than a swelling in the moor which smothers the island (and which makes such a drab frailty of April). It looks perhaps the way Orkney must have in centuries past before that relentless greening began. The only green on a Yell moor in April is a boggy ooze. Yet Yell is the Shetland I carry with me, the Shetland I pack when I leave, the Shetland I am impatient for when I return. It works because of where it is, an island among islands, a perfectly seated lynchpin which makes geographical sense of all Shetland, and without which the whole archipelago would slide out of kilter and slither uncontrollably into the sea. The heart of it is all moor, the seagoing fringe of it relieved only by the stubbornest of crofts (the Shetlander is no Orcadian when it comes to farming); the setting of it all is its jewel, all kaleidoscopic seas bedevilled and beautified by more winds than most places would know what to do with.

That April day, for example, when I stepped from the car travel-crumpled and grateful and walked a downhill pace or two from the road towards Ness of Sound (a tombolo – an outcrop of island like a lollipop attached to its parent island by the stick), the wind had fashioned below me two seascapes from its westerly brushwork. The first was the nearer sea of Yell Sound, which as far as the west wind is concerned lies in the lee of the highest hills of Shetland's north mainland, bluntly and redly crowned by Ronas Hill. In that shelter (a relative term in Shetland implying an absence of perpetual storm) the sea convulsed gently in slow, gray-white shivers, silvering to the north.

That fits. In the landscapes of my mind – those places to which I make notional journeys while my feet are too mainland-locked for too long too far south for comfort – my travels grow brighter as they go north. They silver in the north, like Yell Sound. So I looked down on an April morning and saw on the sound a map of my traveller's inclinations, gray and half moribund and slumbrous among the southmost islands, whitening and stirring and restless in the middle waters impatient for north-ness and light, silvering and shining where the ocean broke about that small and fragmented Thule of Ramna Stacs.

I could generalise and say that northmost means more to me than westmost. Among Highland landscapes I incline first to the Cairngorms, not the northmost in the land but exclusive preserve of the silveriest, northmost sensation of all, the Arctic.

So that was the first of Yell Sound's two landscapes, canny and calm and unfretting its dark and broken shores. The second was in the north, where the light, the water and the island shore lay vivid and uneasy. The two landscapes were divided by a line, a single thick ripple, sprayed by the wind across the Sound from shore to shore, oceanic graffiti. North of that line is also north of the Shetland mainland's northmost headland, beyond which the unrestrained Atlantic holds sway, restless even in its deepest sleep, but mostly hell-bent on removing Yell's north-west coast from the map. It is no coincidence that a little to the south of where that dividing line of landscapes thumps into Yell, the island's only road worth the name embarks on a long, tortuous and tactical withdrawal to the east shore. Nature has the north-west corner of Yell to itself and only the incomprehensible hint of a remnant of an ancient fort confirms that it was not necessarily always so from the beginning of all the island's time. What possessed the fortifiers? What dire circumstances of necessity or misconception commanded that the thing should be built *there* in the open jaw of the storm? Who did they fear that they felt the need of such a gannet-bold outlook on such a vast wedge of ocean? Certainly there has been no rush of humanity to emulate their choice of settlement in the intervening eons. Otter, kittiwake, eider and skarf come to laugh at the incompatability of an island shore and its islanders. The islanders, meanwhile, laugh on the other side of the island, snug around the calm insides of the east-facing voes, places like Mid Yell and Sellafirth in the lee of Fetlar and Unst; and in holts beyond the ken of otters, like the Hilltop Bar, Yell's unforgettably hospitable howff where the crack is good and from time to time the fiddle playing is out of this world. Virtuosi are as thick on the ground in Yell as tirricks on a May morning.

But it is still April on my hillside above the tin-roofed croft where I have flattened a crude holt of my own in the wan grasses and heather, where

I have become over an hour a still element in the first of the sound's two landscapes. This is the holt with the views. It is the first Yell I remember, the view from this spot, this nowhere-on-the-map, and if a time arrives in my life when I am by with this island madness, it will be the last of Yell I remember too. Every kind of Shetland I have ever tasted and taken to is either within reach or within sight, or the sense of it is easily achieved by the shortest journey of a train of thought.

The croft house down the hill is part of it. The first time I stopped here it was because that house was for sale: £12,000 for four stone walls and a tin roof going copper, and three acres of plunging bits of fields which declined from agriculturally marginal at the top to seaweed at the foot. All that, and the great miles-wide slash of two-textured silk that was Yell Sound and its abutting sea. I looked at it all and the island madness had me in the palm of its hand and wrapped round its little finger and it seemed to me then to be a fair image of heaven. I look at it now and it still does. It might as well have been £120,000, of course, but such considerations do not intrude in the minds of the island-fevered when the fever is rooted in such a dream-fertility as a low hillside on Yell just above the sound with April poised to emerge from its shell and dare spring to crack its first smile. Now I was back in Shetland, back on Yell and although the house seemed to have mouldered a bit and the land mouldered a lot at my back, beneath my feet and for all the land and sea and sky miles I could take in, there rose and fell all the contours of all the islands I could ever wish to jostle one pair of eyes in one glance, and all their maternal seas. Yell's sea sucked and blew among the rocks like a half-hearted whale and I put a sigh on the island air of such a wistful power that it probably hangs there still, becalmed in its perpetual April pause.

> On low lowland days
> I would drowse by
> a hearth of dream-kindling,
> would wake in
> the evening of the north.
> There, silken sea-scent prevails
> blown on morning airs
> which lipped Foula
> in their eastering flight.
> The sound would settle
> and still, silver and gray;
> Ramna Stacs would float firm
> as hard smoke;

seals would croon by Uyneray
out-crooned by eiders.

On slow island days
I would light a fire
on a cold and empty hill
would fan a flame
to thwart the hypothermia
of the island's soul.
There I would raise up
old walls, would set down roots
where once they flourished
thick as sheep; my smoke
would call and call all
the old stone-stacking
flame-fanning spirits home.

A stubborn crop
of rock and rush,
wrack and hush
would be my estate.
That tide-tumbling wake
is the otter's –
we would trespass mutually.

A child, hill-heady,
would laugh and listen
through stanzas, songs
and sagas; the spirits
who wrote them would nod
from window seats, while others
heard from the hill,
from the rotting schoolhouse.

That rekindling
would inherit the child;
that first smoke-song
would echo and echo
from a blaze of hearths.

PREVIOUS PAGE: *Sunlight and storm at the mouth of Nibon's
beautiful little sea valley*

On high island days
I would drowse by
a hearth of dreamlessness.
There would be no need
for dreams.

But I am no islander. And while I think I could make a good one (for I love the clearly defined set of landscape circumstances to rework day after day, as I love that good self-containment they know in Stromness when the *Ola* homes in for the weekend), islands like Yell have suffered almost as much from the repopulation by incomers as from the depopulation of their own, and good intentions do not turn an incomer into a son of the island soil. That is not to say there is no place for the incomer and his new life-blood, but in too many of the islands in these pages it is overdone and thoughtlessly overdone and the islands are the poorer for it. Yell still harbours enough Yell voices to be convincing, but there are far fewer than there once were, and a formidable tide must turn here, as elsewhere, if a troublesome imbalance is to be rectified.

So I sat above the otter shore, above the wilting tin roof, and I was as content as I will ever be with the necessarily unrequited nature of my island love, and if I ever redefine my attitude towards islands and islanders and attempt to become an islander myself, somewhere about here would be fine, thank you.

My eyes took in the shore again, working north up the sound, refamiliarising myself with details. There is, for example, a broch down there, or rather what has been a broch before much of the stone of its tall, round walls was hived off to meet the building needs of this civilisation or that, doubtless reworked many times in the 1,400 years or so since the broch-builders turned their backs on the one great architectural phenomenon peculiar to Scotland. This one's site makes more sense than the fort-builders made, but the broch folk were domestic at heart, not warriors, and perhaps less mindful of the whereabouts of foes as a result. Within the broch's ingeniously impregnable strength, they had no need of aggressive tendencies. No weapon of war was ever found on a broch site, not one, just the utensils of domesticity. So the choice of site probably had as much to do with the availability of workable stone as strategic importance, although from the evidence of many of the broch sites I have visited, the builders, whoever they were, had an appreciative eye for nature: the most consistent feature I have seen is natural beauty. The west shore of Yell Sound is not an exception to that rule, even with the land locked in its April-drab. There are always the two seas to flow through each other, trembling the sound even on its

Yell's north-west shore: 'the unrestrained Atlantic holds sway,
restless even in its deepest sleep . . .'

*The astonishing survival of Mousa broch as seen from the ruinous
Burraland broch across Mousa Sound*

rarest, stillest days, a loosely chequered board for the play of the chess-piecing islands advancing and retreating and succumbing in the face of light and shade and storm. And two or three weeks hence, should I still be sitting here, my eye would alight on an erratic, snowflake-flimsy scrap of flight head-winding it up the sound, bouncing on the air, skipping down among the small waves, landing at last in the heart of the broch's decrepit ring, advance-guard of the bird-snow. It would land with a thin, hoarse laugh: 'Tirrick! Tirrick!' and all Shetland stirs at that. It is the return of the arctic tern, not bud or bulb or blink of sun, which finally convinces the islander that winter's throw of the dice is done. There will be another spring now.

My eye fell on the broch again. I tried to furnish its low remnant with something like the astonishing survival of Mousa a few Shetland shores to the south. If I had the time-traveller's ticket to such places I would put myself among these northmost islands 2,000 years ago when they were studded with the boldness of the brochs, to see who lived within them and how. Best guesses are all we have to go on. Ian Hannah, author of the 1934 classic *The Story of Scotland in Stone*, paid them this tribute:

> . . . the famous brochs, those earliest buildings of any note that press our rock-bound soil. Nothing very like them has been found in any other land, and it is at least possible that they influenced our castles till the days of Mary Queen of Scots. Some had apparently been years in use when Christ was born . . . One group is in the far north, with many examples on Orkney, clearly their true home; another is scattered, far less thickly, through the south. Among the works of that great building age their place is high. Even the traveller who had paced the hills of Rome might have beheld their massive though uncultured forms without contempt.
>
> Their round and battering, unwindowed walls are sometimes 19 feet in thickness, and never less than nine; some stand no less than 60 feet in height. Like the Parthenon built dry and with masonry peculiarly well fitted, however rude, they enclose round open courts some 30 feet or more across, and there are mural stairs and chambers sometimes domed, with parapeted walls round their tops, anticipating far less pristine forts.

Mousa puts the flesh on that skeletal account, its round and tapering walls climbing more or less intact to the roofline (although no one is certain there *was* a roof). I prefer to watch it from a distance rather than join a camcording boatload loudly trampling its ancient silence underfoot. The ruinous broch of Burraland across Mousa Sound is a good place, for that low tumbledown emphasises the miracle of Mousa's survival. Distance also lends

Mousa broch a sense of reality, as though it stood again in its own time. Close to, close enough to touch the stones, there is no such thing, although there is instead the marvelling at the skill of the builders, and at the brain which devised such a monumentally functional house, a design so successful and so rooted in its time that it dignified landscapes from here to the Scottish border; not one broch deviated from the carefully reasoned blueprint.

All this unravelled as I tried in my mind to impose a Mousa on Yell's unnamed stony ring. I watched the thing rise, stone on stone, until the first smoke stood above it on just such a still, gray April morning, a flag to denote residents within. You can take such flights of fancy so far. A lobster boat's engine introduced a less-than-Iron-Age note into my reverie, and the broch lay as decrepit and tumbledown and unsmoking as before, but briefly I had superimposed my reference point, my Mousa, on the site, and some sense of the Shetland that was, some new awareness of the broch-builders' art, was mine. It was a valuable insight. It was won by doing what I do best in the islands – sitting still and listening, to the land, to the voices of nature, to the people. It does not do to take your mainlander's prejudices into such places, for different codes hold sway and you are a stranger in their midst. Listen, watch, pay heed, respect what it is which prevails among the Yells of the island world, savour it, and if you would stay, be prepared to don its cloak and shed your own. Put a broch on a shoreline where none has stood for a thousand years by all means, but be patient too in the face of an explanation of why the broch was demolished to rework its stones into a farmhouse, why the farmhouse in turn was allowed to moulder away while a kit bungalow on a concrete raft was built alongside. So you would like the stone croft house with the tin roof. The islander who grew up in such a place would like a house which rebuffs the wind. He is as aware as you are that one is fitting and befits the landscape, and one is not and does not, but when he argues that life is difficult enough here without having to fight his house as well as the weather, depopulation, transport costs, smart-ass incomers, you had better be miraculously persuasive on behalf of archi-tectural tradition or hold your wheesht. I have heard the islanders' argument so often that I have a reluctant sympathy for it, but I have also met some who cherish the tradition and take the trouble to uphold it, and there is nothing reluctant about my sympathies for them.

In the middle of the day, the wind fell away to a profound stillness, a rare enough commodity in the islands of Scotland. In Shetland it is uncanny. A dog bark somewhere over by Lochend on the mainland came bouncing over the sound like a flat stone, well thrown. The lull was almost hallucina-tory. The boat's engine was gone, the sound, south of its ocean-going divide, put reflections under its floating gulls, and you could count on the toes of one webbed foot how often that happens in a year. If I could have harnessed the lull to my broch day-dreaming, who knows what the hour might have contrived, but my mind's eye was adrift now and roving, far across that great organic stillness to where a mesmerism of crackling sunlight threw a yellow splintery tinsel-show about the stubby upstart rocks of Ramna Stacs. It was a quirky, unfathomable trick of light, for the sun shone nowhere else, and even on the stacs it seemed only to ignite highlights, water edges, a canted over face, rock points and angles, phosphorescent scraps, so that I began to wonder if the sun was responsible for the show at all.

The stacs stood line astern from where I sat, coyly peering round the nearest and bulkiest of their small tribe, Gruney. They are a wondrously charismatic gathering, making their own mischief, changing places and realigning themselves as you navigate shore or sound or ocean, whitening their roots as storms muster or banshee-ing weirdly as winds fizz through their jagged gaps and channels. It is a connoisseur's landscape which sets Ramna Stacs for its centrepiece. I have long since acquired the habit of reciting their northward progression almost like a litany: Gruney, Flae-ass, Fladda, Turla, Scorder, Outer Stack, Gaut Skerries. The long-gone crofters of the long-derelict crofts at Uyea on the north shore of the Shetland mainland would know them uniquely, for they would see them against the midsummer sunrise, standing stones of the northern ocean. Children weaned on such elemental symbolism would weave it into their games and never forget where they came from, nor could they fail to know (and without asking) why it is that those famed islandscapes the rest of us thoughtlessly classify from afar as 'heritage' truly matter.

Likewise, the fort-dwellers up the coast, whatever unencumbered tempests they felt it necessary to thole, could set the widest profile of Ramna Stacs against their winter-into-spring sunsets. Perhaps that was why they built where they did, and perhaps my fanciful idea of the stacs as oceanic standing stones was not so fanciful. We were not there. We don't know. But more than once I have seen them harness scraps of sunlight when no other sun shone, and once, too, I saw the lowest of horizon-clinging suns go deftly through the stacs, throwing the shadows of them on to their fellows and across small slabs of becalmed sea. There was something almost holy in the moment and I caught myself litanising the stacs again . . . Gruney, Flae-ass, Fladda, Turla, Scorder, Outer Stack, Gaut Skerries . . . and I wondered by what gutturals the fort-builders knew them.

The sun-fire dowsed, the north sky darkened, the sound's dividing line hardened again, the ocean crumpled, the sound fretted and emptied of its birds, winds stirred and strengthened, and fast curtains were hauled closed among the stacs. At last there was only Gruney left, briefly isolated from

'My affection for islands and my writer's instincts have brought me
closer to Shetland than many a shore . . .' Rare summer
tranquillity off Lerwick harbour

its fellows. A surge of storm whitened its stance while the sky blackened and blurred its recognisable shape to an abstraction, then the storm swallowed it whole. I had the glasses on it as the storm stooped. The stac's last gesture was gloriously futile: it was to fire a salvo of kittiwakes into the storm-cloud's open gape. No one and nothing . . . not the crofters of Uyea nor the fort builders of the Yell shore, not my admiring gaze nor my speculative frame of mind . . . none of these knows Ramna Stacs the way the kittiwake does.

Three weeks later the terns were back. The first of them turned heads all across Shetland. Mine turned across Laxo Voe, where I was sitting, May warmed, head down over a notebook. At that first thin, two-syllable giggle I snatched up the glasses without putting down the pen, and found four arctic terns on a spit of shingle and two more hovering over the shallows. It was at that precise moment, more than any other I have ever known, that I wished I had been born a Shetlander, more particularly a Yell Shetlander. The arctic tern is a world cruiser, flying up and down the globe for a living, thirled addictively to the turning sun, but enough of them choose Shetland for that pivotal pause in their life-cycle to transform utterly its wilder shores. On Yell it has the impact of August on a heather moor, and nothing draws the islander closer to nature's year than the first terns.

As one whose work is forever shackled to the pursuit of a closer bonding of man and nature (and flying in the face of what too often seems to be man's preferred direction) I cannot but be profoundly impressed at this small symbol of the wedding of islander to a rhythm of nature. How much more potent a symbol, though, to see and feel it through an islander's eyes, the islander who has tholed all his life's winters here and knowing neither birch bud nor daffodil nor the loosening of songbird throats, but to be spring-gladdened instead by the arrival of the jaunty flight of arctic terns at the head of a wake which reaches back down half the world's oceans.

My affection for islands and my writer's instincts have brought me closer to Shetland than many a shore. An earlier book, a collaboration with photographer Colin Baxter called *Shetland – Land of the Ocean*, lured me here in the first place and won a few friends among islanders. It also produced a commission from *The Independent* newspaper in January 1993 when the oil tanker *Braer* ran aground in Quendale Bay off the south Mainland. The result was a poem, 'The Long Wait in the Wind':

A LONG WAIT IN THE WIND

It has been a long wait
in the wind, that ill-at-ease
wind of change. Now fear
is laid aside to deal dully with disaster.
But at least we *knew*
about the wait, the wait
and the warning and the wind.
The otters and the birds
knew only the wind.

Ever since our glad hand beckoned
oil ashore at Sullom Voe
we began to wait for its gatecrash
on some wild and unprepared tract –
a reckoning behind our backs. On an island
you can only face one shore at a time.

Today the reckoning
is fastened to Quendale Bay
like a peninsula
and the waiting ones were right:
the oil has not come ashore
at Sullom Voe.

The wind has done this.
They said it would,
the waiting ones, for the wind
permits no lethargies of the soul
for the Shetlander, and varies
only in the degrees of its withering assault.

Life here is a courageous compliance, bowing
to the overlordship of winds,
mourning and singing
to their whims. Today we mourn.
One spring-bright tomorrow
on Ronas Hill, the wind
will eddy the land in song:
we will sing too, and briefly
forget – forget today
and the new waiting
which by then will have begun.

Besides, all Shetland's story
is wrought by winds of change.
This ill-at-ease wind
bore gifts – jobs, roads, ferries,
social vigour, brimming coffers,
and stemmed
that cancerous flow – south! south! –
of our children. Why then
should there not be a price?

And at least we knew
about the wait, the wait
the warning and the wind. But oh!
If only we could have warned
the fish and the birds,
the seals and the otters

and our lovely land.

A year after the *Braer* disaster, a year of many more winds and tankers in trouble and Klondyker ships in worrying numbers – shoals and shoals of them – the newspaper asked to rerun the poem and a sequel entitled 'The Wind That Sulks':

Nature has ripped the headlines from her.
She's yesterday's news, broken,
sunken, shrunken to sea level.
The world has packed and gone to stare
at someone else's *Braer*.

Now I should go back,
now the watcher tides have ebbed
and left behind, quiet in slack water,
the battened-down islanders.
I was absent for the wounding
but should be there for the healing
after the heroics,
enduring, aligned with the stoics.

Besides, I too have grieved
for distance salts the wound of others
in my mind – Shetland and Shetlander,

'If only we could have warned the fish and the birds, the seals and the otters, and our lovely land . . .'

flier and swimmer,
the clean air grown black,
the sea gone deadly slack.

But expert voices claim
'The wind has healed!'
while silent Shetland waits
and fears the unforgiving unrevealed hand
the wind may play, the unpredicted price
to pay. For every enemy
the islands ever knew
who burned and warred
and reefed the coast in hulks
Shetland only ever learned to fear the wind that sulks.

Winds colour all Shetland's shades, the curse of the *Braer*, the blessing of
the terns. I hurried back from Laxo Voe to Yell. There is a roadside pond
near where I sat and watched Yell Sound and its two seas, the same
pond where two years previously I had watched a pair of terns flicker up
from the sea and settle. For an hour they were restless, lifting often on the
cutting edges of their wings, sniping uneasily at each other or anything else
which encroached on their low-lying airspace – a lark, a plover, a pippit.
But after another hour they were sunning, preening, unpacked and restful,
the journey done, or at least as done as any arctic tern's journey is ever
done, a lull between hemispheres. I had sat and sunned myself too, my own
tern-ish restlessness just as comfortably stalled, quietly contented that we –
the terns and I – had washed up on the same fragment of the same island
shore.

Such small gestures of nature matter to me: they reinforce my belief that
there is a better, a closer way to co-exist with our natural surroundings than
the one we have chosen to live as a species . . . which is mostly in opposition
to nature. We have lost the instinct which once governed our lives . . . that
if you take from nature, you must also put back. It is to the great credit of
the Yells of this world that they still have the capacity to remind you.

Now, two years later, I crossed to Yell again and drove north in search
of the pond, daring to hope there would be terns again. I found it much
more easily than I had imagined because in that warm late afternoon the
terns had walked the few yards from the pond and settled down to some
serious sunbathing in the middle of the road.

Chapter Three

A MAP OF AUSTRALIA, GONE GREEN

SHAPINSAY IS THE one which looks like a map of Australia gone green, or if you must (this being Orkney where a characteristic pragmatism frowns on such fancifully romantic analogies) a slightly warped Viking helmet. Besides, as they will tell you on Shapinsay, it's the other way round: Australia is the one which looks like a map of Shapinsay, but they've put Tasmania in the wrong place. They point to Helliar Holm off the south-west corner, not the south-east, and tell you that Orkney was mapped many centuries before Australia, and in the face of such irrefutable evidence you nod sagely, grateful for the establishing of perspectives. Shapinsay from Shapinsay is the centre of the universe and Australia just another island over the horizon, like Fair Isle.

Kirkwall, back down Orkney a bit, across the inevitable sound, is a metropolis to be regarded with a kind of affectionate pity. You see it from the road down to the pier, a gray shapelessness from the midst of which the peak of its cathedral pointedly admonishes the ungodly for miles around, all the way to Westray on a good day. In Kirkwall's close-gathered streets there are few enough opportunities to stand back and admire the vision and the daring and the passion of the grand gesture which built St Magnus Cathedral, but from Shapinsay four miles away, the gesture *is* grand. Even at that distance its biblical bulk outbraves Shapinsay's own rearing stone edifice. You look at Balfour Castle's carbuncular monument to a single Victorian ego and shudder, and you turn and bless from afar the anonymous cathedral builders for their humble genius and whatever manner of God it was which propelled the work upwards.

William Golding's novel *The Spire* is a wondrous insight into all that. His dean, Jocelin, who commands an impossible spire to be built on top of

his cathedral after a vision, tells his master mason:

> The net isn't mine, Roger, and the folly isn't mine. It's God's Folly. Even
> in the old days he never asked men to do what was reasonable. Men
> can do that for themselves. They can buy and sell, heal and govern. But
> then out of some deep place comes the command to do what makes no
> sense at all – to build a ship on dry land; to sit among the dunghills; to
> marry a whore; to set their son on the altar of sacrifice. Then, if men
> have faith, a new thing comes.

The cathedral was a new thing in the middle decades of the twelfth century,
built at the instigation of Earl Rognvald Kolsson and dedicated to his uncle,
the martyr, Magnus, infamously murdered in 1115 on Egilsay. The islanders,
still agog and appalled at the nature of what was done, must have watched
the new thing rise in their midst with a mixture of awe and admiration and
incredulity. The small army of sooth-moother itinerants who came to set
stone on stone and carve crude rejoinders to their gaffers (setting them
mischievously into the great walls, small thorns to torment sanctity) were
just one more invasion of incomprehensible tongues among islands well
accustomed to such things. But the building must have appeared miraculous
even to such instinctively skilled stoneworkers as the Orcadians. Out-by on
Shapinsay they would see the thing grow hugely in certain lights until tower
and blunt spire cut the skyline (the present spire is a twentieth-century
replacement: the purists object; I like it) and the shape of Orkney was
changed for ever.

Shapinsay performs for Orkney the function which Yell holds down in
Shetland, a centrepiece, but it does it better, for although there is no sense
of a lynchpinning presence nailing the whole island mass to the ocean like
Yell does, and although Shapinsay is a stepping-stone to nowhere, it lies in
the crook of the Orkney mainland's elbow, and from what passes for high
ground you look out through every compass point bar a few either side of
west at a bewilderment of island shapes, a primeval scattering, a shoal
of islands with whaleback streamlining, carved and curved by winds and
tides. The islander is confident with names and shapes and distances. The
incomer, or the fly-by-night tripper, is never so certain. And just as the Yell
shore realigns Ramna Stacs for you, so the islands swim puzzlingly among
each other, cutting off each other's Noups and Nesses and Heads and Holms

*PREVIOUS PAGE: The 'biblical bulk' of St Magnus Cathedral in
Kirkwall seen from Shapinsay*

as you journey up and along and down Shapinsay's low-slung spine. Fog can turn the game into a hypnotic magic . . .

. . . I parted the curtain of the Ferry Inn at Stromness on to a shroud, Orkney in an autumn dawn, fogbound and dripping. What was not gray was white. The air was soaking although nothing was falling you would call rain. The natives looked heedless enough of it in the street (wall-to-wall pavements, traffic backing off for pedestrians, a good regime) but they were dissecting it endlessly in shops, cafés, doorways. On an island, the weather is God, the more so because as you move around it, especially when it has Orkney's limitless sprawls of sky, you can see it coming, arriving, departing. Fog not only blots out the islands in Orkney, it blots out the weather too. Orkney shuts its door on the fog, and turns its hospitable back. Fog threatens the safe passage of boat and plane, and in their absence Orkney draws itself in like a snail which has seen the orange-prowed advance of an oystercatcher.

But the nature writer must work with all nature's moods, which is as benevolent a euphemism as I can muster for an Orkney fog. I tried to think of somewhere to go which might somehow be enhanced by the shroud, somewhere hard-edged perhaps which the blurring of the fog might briefly soften. I thought of Brodgar.

The Ring of Brodgar in a fog is the stones without a context, the ring reduced to an arc, half a dozen stones at any one glance. The great signposting stones of Stenness (a kind of gateway as I see it) were standing shadows, uneasily adrift, unrooted. On a clear day, Stenness Loch seems to stretch unbroken clear over to Hoy's hills. In the fog it reached no further than a colourless heron twenty yards offshore, a garden-centre shape contemplating its own equally colourless upended twin with which it shared the same pair of legs. Swans drifted in and out of the fog, creatures of myth and dream, emblematic of the three Norse Fates – Past, Present and Future – crossing and recrossing in and out of the visible world. Island fog does this, easing the passage of the mind through seas of incredulity so that you look as in a theatre, the stage and the drama moving as you move, continually redefining and reinventing itself. At Stenness there was a cast of swans, a walk-on part for a heron, and the gaunt, towering Watch-Stone (a heron-solitary totemesque giant guarding the causeway between two lochs). It would be a dull soul which leaned his nonchalance against the stone and watched swans swimming to and from the foggy void and failed to fall prey to a fermentation of feynesses. I barged through the half mile of fog to Brodgar with the strength of the Watch-Stone in me and the fateful swan-gods airborne in my mind. Their stage set moved with me, always ahead, always curtained. I would confront Brodgar and demand knowledge, understanding, insight, imposing the memory of earlier seasons on the fog-theatre.

*Shapinsay lies in the crook of the Orkney mainland's elbow ...
you look out from the high ground to a primeval scattering of
far island shapes*

OPPOSITE: *'I tried to think of somewhere to go ... somewhere hard-
edged perhaps which the blurring of the fog might briefly soften. I
thought of Brodgar'*

Hear me, Brodgar! (Brodgar was a battalion of shadows: there was no sense of its mighty ring in the fog-gloom, no hint of hearing in its muteness.)

Declare yourself, Brodgar! Who? Why? What is your meaning? I have stood between Watch-Stone and swan-fates! Enlighten! (No! Wait! That's done it now . . . that gauntlet's six millennia too late for comfort!)

No! I will not go out there and stand at the hub of your Ringing – I dare not! – turning sunwise, unravelling meaning stone by stone for fear (for what unnameable fear?) of your enlightenment; for fear revelation would amount to too toilsome a burden!

Hold still with your stones, Brodgar. The way you realign them as I walk, erase them at my back like swan-gods at Stenness . . . are you in league with Ramna? Are you the same stone-stoic tribe? Do you plumb the same depths of land as Ramna thrusts down to its ocean-bed anchor? (The same silence, the same profound illiteracy, the same unanswering fog-binding.)

Ignore my hollow bravado, Brodgar! My thrown gauntlet relies on your deafness for its effect. We both know that if you rose now, Brodgar, beckoning from the heart of your own interred concentric circle within and spread before me a blueprint elucidating all, I would stammer back inconsequentialities we'd both disown!

Wait though, Brodgar. If by chance my swan-fancies ever steer me so that we share the same Valhalla, and my eyes are unobscured by the dulling cataracts of my awe, show me then. I will talk eagerly and wisely in the face of your spread blueprint then.

It was a slow, blindfolded progress through the island to Kirkwall and the Shapinsay ferry, no discernible difference in the motion of car and ferry, the waters of Kirkwall Bay and The String as flat and firm and empty as Orkney's roads. But beyond the bay, a change had begun. Beyond the starboard headland there lay the one everyday phenomenon of nature this of all days had done without: distance. At the end of that distance lay an island, small and alone and miraculously lit, so low to the sea that its lighthouse (tall as a white standing stone) made it look top-heavy: Auskerry.

There was also a vertical distance. Something clearly definable as sky was emerging in ripples and creases above which stood stains of brightness, brightness and colour which startled simply because it was there. Some meteorological mischief was unwrapping the northern isles of Orkney piece-meal. Shapinsay, which had been as invisible as the rest of the world from Kirkwall, was suddenly in on the colouring conspiracy, alight and green and vivid, and roping in the reluctant hill shades of Rousay, yet still where there should have been Wyre and Egilsay there lay the Brodgar shroud, low on the water as homing droves of gannets.

Shapinsay was barely believable sunlight. Hurry away from the castle and its incongruous wood, uphill and on to the island's long and languorous spine. Stop now and breathe in the difference. Look around you. All is below. See how your world has been redefined. Islands are relative. From Scotland, Orkney is outlandish, a nomadic cluster of islands which moves around the weather map, although not as nomadic and movable as Shetland. (A Shetlander once told me, in a bar in Stirling of all places, that he and his fellow islanders thought they had learned to be philosophical at the liberties map-makers take with Shetland until a television programme inexplicably accommodated it in a box in the Solway Firth. 'That was a new one on all of us,' he said, 'so I wrote to the television programme and congratulated them. I told them it was amazing the improvement in the weather since we were shipped sooth t' the Saalway, what with the Gulf Stream and all those palm trees takkin root in the street.')

Orkney usually winds up somewhere off the Dornoch Firth which is at least on the way, but once you set foot on where the place really is as opposed to where the map-makers would have you believe it is, there is more of a sense of a 'mainland' island and 'the rest' than there is in Shetland. The geography of the two island groups has as much to do with that as anything, but Shetland's extra distance up the northern ocean and its more blatantly enduring Norse instincts are a profoundly unifying force. Orkney's northern islands, especially, proclaim their individuality, their exclusive charismas. From Shapinsay (which is neither mainland nor a truly northern isle) you see them for what they are, a scatter of jigsaw-piece shapes which don't fit anything other than their own ragged-edged niche in their own sundered sea. From most viewpoints among 'the rest', Kirkwall is . . . well, it's school and shopping and sometimes it's work, but ach, man . . . traffic wardens! Stromness is where you go to catch the boat to Scotland and much good may it do you. Shapinsay (a brave man from such as Westray or Sanday or North Ronaldsay might say) is practically mainland, but he would be foolhardy to mouth such an utterance on Shapinsay. Those four seaward ferryboat miles are innocuous enough to the Papa dweller or the day tripper, but to the Shapinsay native they distinguish between Orkney and the promised land.

I have some sympathy with that opinion. Even when you stand off Kirkwall as close as Shapinsay, you feel the drawbridge rising at once at your back, the moat widens and deepens – but benevolently – you draw breath and inhale a more profound island-ness. If you encounter it as I did for the first time just as Orkney has began to unwrap itself from the Brodgar shroud, you see a wing-flexing butterfly of islands shaking off its chrysalis, and you are grateful to Shapinsay forever because nowhere else in all Orkney is so well placed for such a revelation.

'He surfaced and paused twenty yards offshore, chins rolling down to his chest, standing in the water like a gray iceberg . . .'

So I had stopped on Shapinsay's roof, which is really not much higher than its ground floor: like much of Orkney, it's a single-storey island. But that small elevation unfurls much of the island beneath you, a vivid spread-eagle of green turning yellow in the lowering autumn sun. Autumn is perhaps the perfect time for such a perfect viewpoint, for it is then that any northern island landscape disports itself in more shades than at any other season. Orkney's all-pervasive green is softened by the sun's yellowing, the few remaining heather hills and moors are darkening from purple to brown, the sea is all the colours a sea can be from gray-white back towards the mainland to deep royal blue off Shapinsay's north coast to sky blue out where Auskerry ripples the eastern horizon, and all across the firths of Stronsay and Westray there are tricks of green and silver and blue and gray as the retreating mist dances to the tune of the sun. As the mist relents over the islands, and the sun lights what has been an unseen landscape, the land shades glow pastel green and yellow behind the mist. Islands appear where there were none. That white beach far to the north-east must be Sanday (you murmur, 'Oh, a Sanday beach') and the islander, who has heard the joke before, perhaps a thousand times, raises his eyes.

The Mor Stane, Shapinsay: 'lavished with the attention of suns and all the island's winds, baring its soul to the moon . . .'

The last to clear are Wyre, birthplace of the poet Edwin Muir, and Egilsay, deathplace of St Magnus. The martyrdom of Magnus in 1116 was the Shapinsay of Orkney history, the central reference point which makes sense of all the rest. The breath of Magnus and the breath of Orkney are one and the same. The history books (including the most astonishing history book of them all, *The Orkneyinga Saga*) spell out the bare bones of that unique relationship, but it takes a poet, George Mackay Brown, to put flesh on the story. His novel, *Magnus*, is one of the few modern books acclaimed as classics which have a right to bear that distinction. The breath of Magnus and the breath of Orkney course through the writing in the same fluent stream, and neither the cause of the martyr nor the islands was ever served better.

A rainbow moved ahead of a far northern showering. A hint of memory sends fingers fumbling through my books, B for Brown. I find what I am looking for, a poem called 'Orkney: The Whale Islands':

> . . . A rainbow crumbled
> Over Orc, 'whale islands'.
> Then the skipper, 'The whales
> Will yield this folk
> Corn and fleeces and honey'.
> And the poet,
> 'Harp of whalebone, shake
> Golden words from my mouth'.

One of the purest satisfactions of islands a writer might glean amid such a stubble of islands as Orkney (a shorn crop of the sea's harvesting) is the way circles have a habit of completing themselves. I choose to put it down to the fact that in places at least (and Shapinsay is one such) the rhythm of nature's cycle is still audible and adhered to in the way the land is worked. There, for example, was my rainbow, there the George Mackay Brown poem which drew together the elements of rainbow, the explanation of Orkney as 'whale islands', and a poet's invocation to Orkney as muse. There, as I walked out along Shapinsay's north-eastering spur with a school of whaleback island shapes for my horizons, was the headland called Ness of Ork. The writer who treks landscapes for a living alights on such moments with the glee of an oystercatcher on a mussel bed, glad he has washed up on such a shore.

But that was no whaleback on the seaward edge of the tide-bared rocks of Ness of Ork, for although it broke the water in a low, dark curve and snorted at intervals, it lay on a submerged rock (which no whale willingly does) and for all its tremulous bulk it was many times too small for the smallest of orcs. It was a bull Atlantic seal, monster enough for me at such close quarters, and oblivious to my cautious step-by-step approach across the seaweed-slick rocks. I began photographing him at thirty feet, just the whaleback of him, low in the water as Egilsay. At twenty feet, his head suddenly reared atop an array of chins, his snort was a roar, and with a turn of speed which could have been terrifying if it had been aimed shorewards instead of seawards, and a splash which would not have shamed the *QE2*, he was launched. The small bay echoed to him, a squadron of shear-watering skarfs deferred to the spectacle and rose and diverted well out to sea. He surfaced and paused twenty yards offshore, chins rolling down to his chest, 'standing' in the navy-blue water like a gray iceberg, watching, floating like a cork. Some cork. Then he was gone and swimming energetically north for the Green Holms, which are sealish kinds of places a few leagues up the Stronsay Firth. I watched him go, envying him the particular seagoing knowledge of Orkney he must possess, his familiarity with the very island roots of the seabed, where the islands appear, not as whalebacks but soaring towers, imponderable brochs for a tribe of giants, perhaps.

Shapinsay has another claim to fame. It has *one* standing stone, a source of some pride, affection and a kind of casual familiarity among islanders, almost as if they might pause crossing the crown of the island to pass the time of day with it. I found it late in the afternoon, a shade between yellow and copper in autumn's lowest sunlight, poised between sunset and moonrise, solitary on its heather moor and unnervingly close to the island tip. Its high solitude compounds its mystery, its impact on its small island setting as momentous in its unsung way as the sung ways of Brodgar or Callanish are on theirs. I fancied that if chance should ever turn me into a Shapinsay dweller, I would have that stone for a friend, visiting it often, troubling its tranquil poise with the same pestering inquisition.

Standing
keep stone secrecies
more mute
than swans

Scanning
from whose elevation
secrecies more deep
than oceans

Standing
I offer up my one
recurrent monumental
question

– '?'

The best tribute to the stones and their builders that I have ever come across is the writer Marion Campbell's. Her academic grasp of the ancients is loosened by the soul of a poet, and at times she writes like an angel.

> Ever since the art of erecting them was lost men have been awed by the stones; tales of giants or witches tossing them across valleys, of Sunday dancers frozen in their tracks, of Merlin raising Stonehenge with the power of music, all pay tribute to a lost skill. Now as they stand in rings or in rows, in groups like gossiping giants or in lonely dignity to mark some trackway or grave, we are awed anew by the calculations that dictate their settings. I like to think of the designers – a caste of learned priests, a dynasty of mathematical geniuses? – who drew their plans on the earth and then sat by some camp-fire among the great stones, waiting for moonrise and cracking their little donnish jokes above beakers of honey wine. The stones stand to their memory, but the zest of them is lost.

That 'zest' is a thoughtful word. The Mor Stane (which is how Shapinsay's folk refer to their one stone) is a zesty kind of place, lavished with the attentions of suns and all the island's winds, baring its stone soul to the moon, whitening to the occasional salted snows, fingerpost to the island's newest inhabitants, a wheen of wintering geese which cohabit among the winter grasses and the stubbles with the old-established whooper swans. The island farmers watch the geese with a certain caution. They are by and large, like all Orcadians I have met, possessed of a healthy respect for nature and good at practising a kind of instinctive co-existence. But the geese are new, and although the numbers are not troublesome yet, they watch warily and wonder. There is a very effective island grapevine from Muckle Flugga to Ailsa Craig. They know all about Islay on Shapinsay.

I have no such reservations about geese, but then I'm not an island farmer. I grew up loving them on Tayside, and the sound of them chortling low over the Mor Stane is simply one more grace note on the score of Shapinsay's small symphony of sea and rock and swelling grassland and cap of matt moorland and all Orkney's merry-go-rounding islands adrift around

*'It is that sky, more than the sea, more than the island profiles . . .
which speaks to me most fluently of Orkney'*

the compass and a sky the size of a continent which always looks so outsized for such a small gathering of small islands, but which when you look at it all long enough and hard enough, always fits perfectly.

It is that sky, more than the sea, more than the island profiles, more than the green whalebacks, more than the zest of the stones, more than all of them put together, which speaks to me most fluently of Orkney. It has (as I fancy it) a taller reach than other skies, a wider embrace, a blue curve of infinity. If there is a heaven, I hope its skies are as good as Orkney's. No shade is beyond it, no trick of mirage or meteorology. It tosses storms the way you or I toss peanuts, you see them coalesce, you see them career through sounds, ride roughshod over the low land, charge on over sea after sea aboard their helpless winds, then you see that sky tame the ocean at the storm's back and all Orkney is glittering and quiet and renewed. Zest is a good word for the Orkney landscape under its sky.

Try and photograph it, or draw or paint it, as thousands have tried before you with every shade of despair and distinction, and you catch yourself composing helplessly with two-thirds sky, or three-quarters or seven-eighths: so often that is the nature of Orkney spectacle, so often there is little in the land or the sea which outshines the sky. It is no place for agoraphobics, although even the most ardent hankerer after the spaces of nature will crave a day or two's respite after over-exposure to Orkney's clear-skied extremes. He will not be disappointed, and sooner rather than later, for the next storm or shroud is rarely far behind the last one. But his land-locked heart will soar again if he happens to be crossing to Shapinsay the day Orkney's sky happens to be unpicking the Brodgar shroud. Having envied the bull seal for its familiarity with Orkney's diving dimension, he will turn his head to throw an admiring glance after a skein of whooper swans for their autumn migration cuts its furrow through the northern skies on the edge of the jet stream, and he would know Orkney's sky the way they do.

Chapter Four

'IN GALILEES
OF SKY'

YOU WILL HAVE seen the stone stand. You will have seen it on the shore at Ness of Ork packed into tiers or sliced up in crazy parallel diagonals. You will have seen it in the hunkered-down streets and alleys of Stromness piled meticulously as dark, ragged bricks to build exquisitely functional houses, capable of wading into the sea, just as the seabed rock of Ness of Ork wades out of it. I wrote a poem about Orkney rock once, and when my great friend of ancient Orcadian stock George Garson ('I've heard tell there used to be as many Garsons in Orkney as there are coopats in a field o' coos') wrote a deft and delectable wee book on the islands with all the zest of a standing-stone-erector, he borrowed the poem – 'Orkney All the Way Through' – and named the book after it, a compliment which was better than a fee. This was it:

> Orkney rock is stacked
> and stashed away like fishboxes
> disassembled only
> by the fingering, punching sea.
>
> Split and hewn it makes
> staunch and stubborn dykes
> sea-wall benches
> and wind-wise gables
>
> or stands obediently
> in tombstone wafers; sometimes
> it takes on a life of its own
> and gathers in unearthly parliaments

at Brodgar or Stenness
debating eternity's laws.
Cut it and it letters 'Orkney'
all the way through.

The tombstone wafers flick past on a brisk walk out from Stromness head-on into the west wind along the north shore of Hoy Sound. They stand in a walled burial ground well-flecked with spume when the tide runs and the wind has its dander up, humble and apt among the later vulgar imports fae sooth – angels, urns, columns. They split wondrously thin, the wafers, so thin you might think an Orkney wind would pass clean through, and the sculptor's adze might be in danger of engraving both sides of the stone at once. Split them thinner still, and in squares, and you have huge stone roof tiles. It was the tradition hereabouts for centuries until it died the death of convenience, but here and there it lingers, and here and there all across Orkney, the islanders are rediscovering how to build and restore the way their forebears did. The sense of place again: the well-built house wall is packed with the ends of shallow stones. It mimics the shoreline rock with its packed tiers. Out in the sound, one of Orkney's endless litany of shipwrecks, blockships, scuttled ships and other maritime casualties leans darkly up out of the water, bow and foredeck offering up one more angular echo of the shore rocks: they too cut up under the sea's restless bullying into dark-prowed diagonals.

But the same diagonals offer succour as well as sinister effigies of unforgotten wars. Where the rock splits, even when it is the sea which splits it, it breaks evenly in regular shapes with hard, straight edges and wide, sloping ledges like askew steps. On one brilliant and billowing day of April, these ledges seemed to bulge with fat pale-gray swathes of something like raw cotton. They were strewn over two hundred yards of shore, snug among the leeward edges, but I could make no sense of them and the small, tremulous movements which fluttered about their edges. I put the glasses on them from a leeward shelter of my own and found not broken bales of cotton but hordes of birds, a dense flock of dunlin, thousands of birds, but splintered into groups hundreds-strong, each group packed tight as stones in a Stromness gable and bedded down in the lee of the only shelter they could find on that shore, the inches-deep ledges of the tide-spared rocks.

PREVIOUS PAGE: 'Out in the sound, one of Orkney's endless litany of shipwrecks, blockships, scuttled ships and other maritime casualties leans darkly up out of the water, an angular echo of the shore rocks . . .'

There they stood, storm-stymied, the wind ruffling the feathers of the outermost birds of each group, but the birds at the centre of each throng as snug as it was possible to be on such a shore on such a day. It was then that I began to look closer at the shore and saw that it bore all the hallmarks of a night of storm. I had spent it contentedly in Stromness's Ferry Inn, well fuelled with Highland Park and something called sticky toffee pudding in butterscotch sauce, and all that after the main course which came on Desperate Dan sized platters. Occasionally you stumble across such places in the islands, seafaring howffs where the bar conversation crackles in a dozen tongues, and the same long, dark and windowless room accommodates lounge, pool table and top-class restaurant in the same amicable ambience, and no one much minds whether you wear cocktail dress or wellies or both. So while I had been blissfully battened down for the night, the sea had been leaping about the knees of the Old Man of Hoy and throwing wrack and wreckage about the shores of the sound. What kind of night it had been for a seven-inch slip of a wader bird pinned down on the edge of the ocean is beyond the scope of my imagination or yours. Now in the buoyant morning after, the sea still gorged creamily all along Orkney's west-facing shores, but the sun was hoisting up and round the wall of the blue sky-dome, and as the poet George Mackay Brown put it (writing on his Stromness kitchen table),

a lark splurges in Galilees of sky

And with that splurge in my ear, that wind in my face, that sun at my back, Orkney on either hand and sky everywhere I turned, I was unstoppable. Spring days of such vitality communicate their energy to all naturally motivated forms, and even a walking man can tap its sources. I wanted to walk forever, for the walking had become not just a means of moving but a means of seeing, sensing, scenting, tasting. Every sense was heightened by the surge of natural forces, and to be walking alone on an Orcadian shore at such a moment was to know the privilege of being. I walked as if a small motor was embedded in the small of my back, pushing me through a tunnel in the wind. I had half an idea what it felt like to be that spindrift-sleek fulmar hurdling the shore, body-swerving past me with a fast and side-headed curiosity, cramponing up a cliff, stalling by a ledge, turning on its heel without touching down, dashing downwind, spinning again in its own length and stiffening pencil wings to glide back in a long, shallow dive to the wavetops. The Icarus in me preened himself and said, 'I could do that', but then the bird leaped up the sea air to fend off a cruising bonxie, and in the chase which followed with its breakneck bravado, I recognised my

Hoy Sound and 'all the hallmarks of a night of storm . . .'

'At last it materialised from its impeccable camouflage into an eider duck sitting on her nest, a sumptuous cushion plucked from her own down . . .'

limitations and walked on, exhilarated and contentedly earthbound.

Birds were everywhere that morning. Some were refugees of the storm like the dunlin, sitting tight, not daring to believe the thing was done. A stroppy, arrowhead phalanx of starlings beat up a corner of one small, dyked-in field to put to flight a small squadron of goldfinches. They had been thistle-sifting for seeds, but now they put a new loose knot of colour on the giddy day. They rose fast, a dozen pairs of lance-corporal-striped wings (canary-bold stripes of yellow) buoying up their black and white and brown and scarlet charms into the wind which at once threw the whole formation eastwards into chaos. Any sparrowhawk or harrier working the fields would have profited effortlessly from the moment but there was only a kestrel (a vole-and-beetle hunter, not a birder) head-downing and hanging wings-and-tail-a-twitch, facing down the wind, harnessing it to his bidding. The old name is 'windhover'. I think 'kestrel' is not an improvement.

The bird side-slipped off the wind and cut away east, low and controlled, and as I followed it in the glasses I saw the sea behind it, broken and clawing up at the falcon. Lower and lower the bird flew, between wavetops at times, but with the unerring confidence of one well accustomed to the task, cutting the corner across a small bay to a favourite perching post on a fence. There he sat and looked round, lifted yellow claw to yellow mandible, and picked it clean of some salty irritation. It is characteristic of nature in such a land of so many quicksilver moods as Orkney that it teaches a falcon to fly like a fulmar.

The headland climbed to a bald, blunt pate, all but grassless and polished by endless vigours of wind. Here the sky added yet another dimension, one I had encountered before only on the high plateau lands of the Cairngorms: it curved on down below the land on either side. In such a circumstance you sense briefly that you live on a round planet. Most of Orkney's heart-stopping moments derive from its skies.

I sat on a small ledge where the worst excesses of wind and rain had cracked open the skin of the headland and dropped a piece of the slope perhaps twenty inches, leaving a bare, brown, rock-and-earth step. The place was high enough to see for miles, the day clear enough to add almost infinite distance. The hill's crouch at my back bore the wind's brunt. Far seas sparked whitely amid their deep, dark blues. I unpacked lunch, and as I did so I realised I had been there before – there, on that precise ledge, unpacking lunch. It was the previous June, and I had sauntered south on a hot morning down the coast from Yesnaby, gawping at sea stacs rising from a flat calm. I had climbed the headland for the same kinds of reasons, admired its stance in that low-slung landscape, and found the same ledge. I had been sitting there for perhaps ten minutes when I realised I was not alone. There was an eye, black and watchful, close to the ground a dozen yards away. It took several moments of hard staring to define the shape which held the eye, but at last it materialised from its impeccable camouflage into an eider duck sitting on her nest, a sumptuous cushion fashioned from her own plucked down. She was quite alone, the ledge offered all the shelter she needed and she had no intention of moving. I gathered my half-eaten lunch, photographed her twice, wished her a successful hatching and left.

And now I had rediscovered the same ledge, by accident and from the opposite direction. And now, examining the ground, I puzzled over her choice of nest site. The sea, by the shortest route, was up the headland a few yards then over the edge of a 300-foot cliff. The longer route, by which she would have to lead her brood as soon as they could walk, was a quarter of a mile of steep slope and foreshore with not a scrap of shelter to thwart the bonxies and the big gulls. Still, doubtless she had her reasons. I wondered how she had fared and whether, a month or two from now, she would fly up from the sea, put down on the slope beside me, cross to my ledge, and without pausing to admire the view, begin to pluck at her own breast.

Birds are forever exercising your mind in Orkney.

Anything-but-mute swans
cram the loch, thick as ripples.

Whaup and peesie choirs
drench Brodgar's Ring
in a huge croon.

Rook foliage
thickens the few trees
and land-lover windhover haunts the tide.

There are so many birds in Orkney
because there is so little land.

Sea-maa screams
catch in their own throats
choked by brutal bully-bonxies.

Cliff-fuls of kittiwakes
chant that tireless lightsome
nom-de-plume.

Fulmars sleekly slice
through the thermaled ease
of lazier throngs while

Hoy's mile-high eagle
lords it over the cluttered scope
of all their lower horizons.

There are so many birds in Orkney
because there are so many skies.

I walked back down on to a flank of the headland, the turf cropped and
blown smooth, the wind bouncing up the cliffs and blaring into geos
and gloups and other concessions the land has reluctantly made to the
inevitable sea. It was in that brash and bare place that I came on one more
derelict farmstead. It wore the usual air of abject disconsolation, it spoke
with the usual tones and vocabulary of sorrow, it stank with the usual
stench of sheep. I was as repelled by its decay as I was magnetised by its
relict and confident survival, as enraged by what its decay stood for as I

was enchanted by how its survival stood. The usual conflict.

Two things made this one different from other island derelictions.

One was where it stood with its back to the west wind and the green
hill of the headland, its blinded windows focused south-east down Hoy
Sound. Hoy's hills (the most un-Orkney of islands with its close gathering
of high silhouettes) were heaped darkly in the south and the sky went up
over them and round them and on and on forever.

The second characteristic of the place was that to my untutored eye it
seemed to be particularly beautifully built out of a shade of tawny sandstone
which glowed in that brilliant born-again sunlight. The cottage seemed too
new for dereliction, its low and shallow-pitched stone roof intact and snug
inside its gables, its walls the near perfect consummation of that meticulously
packed building tradition of these islands. But the windows were glassless
and the door was off and burned, the floor was carpeted with the shit of
sheep, years of it. The other buildings were further gone, but here and there
around the place, between walls round a gable, under a low lintel, you
would catch a glimpse of the cottage from a distance and that distance would
make it look eerily habitable.

George Mackay Brown (again – who else ever lived so hand-in-glove
with Orkney's spirit?) has a poem called 'Dead Fires'. It was written for the
sea valley of Rackwick on Hoy which has also illumined many of his stories,
but it is no less appropriate to my headland. Its theme is the valley's derelict
crofthouses and the pathos of their lost lives. Three verses at the heart of
the poem say this:

> The three-toed pot at the wall of Park
> Is lost to woman's cunning.
> A slow fire of rust eats the cold iron.
>
> The sheep drift through Reumin all winter.
> Sheep and snow
> Blanch fleetingly the black stone.
>
> From that sacred stone the children of the valley
> Drifted lovewards
> And out of labour to the lettered kirkyard stone.

OPPOSITE: *A traditionally built and traditionally ruinous Orkney
farmstead: 'I was as repelled by its decay as I was magnetised by its
relict and confident survival . . . the usual conflict'*

There is an extraordinary island-ness to George Mackay Brown's work. He writes with a disarming purity of language, a prose style as unspectacular and subtle and elemental as Orkney. But its themes are rooted in a faultless bedrock and it wears lightly an enveloping cloak as seamless and profound as an Orcadian sky. His writing was a head-spinning brew when I first encountered it, aged about twenty. I loved it from the first sip. My head had been turned by the title of *An Orkney Tapestry* and by its cover: even then I was a sucker for a ruinous cottage in a beautiful landscape. What I read within did as much as anything to confirm in me the awakening notion that my embryonic journalism should nurture a writer's ambitions. George Mackay Brown's example also taught me the worth of a sense of place, crucially as an ingredient in writing, and more generally as a way of shaping attitudes towards landscape. As the landscapes of nature have become almost the religion of my life, it is a substantial debt I owe the man.

A few years ago I met him for the first time in the company of our mutual friend, the same George Garson. He emerged from a neighbour's house as we knocked on his door. He said, 'Hello boys.' We shook hands and followed him into his house. I felt like a schoolboy in the company of Roy of the Rovers. I doubt if I contributed a worthwhile sentence to the hours of conversation, but oh how I listened! What I heard was the speech of islands.

If Orkney had a voice, it would sound like George Mackay Brown.

Chapter Five

'VERY PLEASANT DID THOSE ISLAND HILLS APPEAR . . .'

Mull was astern,
Rum on the port,
Eigg on the starboard bow

ROBERT LOUIS STEVENSON'S lyric to the tune of 'The Skye Boat Song' swam into my daydream a few hundred feet above the mountains of Rum. It was late May. Rum was blue. Eigg was as astern as Mull for I was bound not for Skye but the Western Isles, on a British Airways flight from Glasgow to Benbecula.

The Sea of the Hebrides shone and in that mood these islands are the most seductive place on earth. The Western Isles sunbathed, low-lying on their own horizon, glowing darkly. I felt my own pang of longing as Skye slipped below the starboard wing. Longing for Skye is a semi-permanent condition from which I suffer, by which I am blessed. Passing it by was never easy for me. I thought of that different species of longing from which Stevenson suffered. His 'Skye Boat Song' evoked not just a landscape but also his lost youth and the pain of exile. The three lines which complete the verse above are these:

Glory of youth
Glowed in his soul,
Where is that glory now?

He was in the South Seas by the time he wrote that, nursing himself through frequent lapses in his health. But islands establish their own rules, common to all islands. It is the most natural of thought progressions to sit pen-in-

Rum and Eigg, matchless in the west: 'memory locks islands into place more surely than other landscapes . . .'

hand on Samoa and invoke Skye and the islands which drifted astern during a childhood voyage there. Scotland, whether Skye or Swanston, was never far from his thoughts and he wrote of it from half a world away both lyrically and accurately. Wistfully too, for he had the melancholy of the exile at his disposal and wielded it as a tool, capable of exquisite workmanship.

> Give me again
> All that was there,
> Give me the sun that shone.
> Give me the eyes,
> Give me the soul,
> Give me the lad that's gone.

Longing is a constancy of island lore and literature and song partly because so many islanders have been compelled to leave, partly because so many visitors have been bewitched and crave return. Memory locks islands into place more surely than other landscapes. Rum drifted below me and I remembered . . .

. . . Mallaig is a frontier town at dawn. It keeps frontier-town time, which means that at any hour of the day or night it has at least one eye open. At 5 a.m. in mid-April the quayside had been awake for hours. Many boats were being readied. Gear was stowed, cargoes hefted and hauled through well-practised routines. Crewmen bantered. A fag glowed in the shadow of a fo'c'sle. A light irritation of rain danced away inland and the air dried out on its winds.

That bleary straggle of overburdened sleepwalkers stowing rucksacks and tents were the unpractised passengers. Islanders on a ferry home look like part of the furniture, but strangers are too loud, too high on the adrenaline of adventure, or in this case, too tired. The ritual of a 6 a.m. departure after a night of travelling to Mallaig from wherever is a tricky feat of acclimatisation. No one is convincing first time. It was my first time.

We sailed. The sun rose astern of Mallaig's hillside and hopes soared with it. Two islands hardened out under the dark sky of the west. One was low and culminating in a single rampant rock at one end like a rhino horn, and that was Eigg and its Sgurr. The other was an altogether bulkier realm, a compact marshalling of mountains – Rum. There are four 'Small Isles' but only these two put an instantly recognisable imprint on their particular horizon. Canna and Muck are cannier.

I was one of five, a rare mob-handed occasion among my island-going expeditions, caught in a plot hatched late at night in the newspaper office where I worked. Two days on Rum and we were reduced to a quartet. The victim pleaded food poisoning and went home. I say he was a seer and had had a vision of the weather. On the fifth day, we four survivors squelched back to the pier no wiser about the nature or even the shape of Rum than we had been when we arrived.

The first night was in tents. We pitched in watery sunlight. It was the last we would see of the sun until it mocked our homeward wake. Water, however, there would be in excess. The next three days and nights were in a bothy, a snug little howff called Dibidil. Snug, that is, in the way that Noah's Ark was snug, so indistinguishable were the gray variables which represented sea, land and sky. The maps suggested the bothy was perched between mountain and sea. Our eyes told us nothing of the kind. Sea and sky and mountain were a meaningless fusion, a porridge of wet rock. We walked coastal paths and saw no coast, climbed into corries and saw no mountains. We sat before hissing fires and drank tea and whisky and ate and shivered while our clothes steamed.

The bothy logbook suggested the experience was by no means rare. I was flexing the new-found muscle of my poetry in those days, brandishing it brazenly and none too selectively. I now wrote a four-line verse in the book, much as Burns (as I fancied it) would casually scratch lines on the window of a favoured hostelry. I would write a miniature masterpiece so pregnant with wit and island wisdom that it would be enshrined forever in the literature of Rum. Having written it, I flicked back through the book and found many poems. The prevalent common characteristics were their subject matter (the weather) and their awfulness. On one page I found three poems by three different hands. They shared the page with a fourth hand which complained tersely: 'The four curses of Rum – rain, wind, midges and poets.' I carefully tore my page from the book. It burned well.

'Share the joke, Sir?'

It seems I had been smiling to myself when the steward arrived with the coffee. I grinned, pointed down.

'Rum,' I said, 'long story.'

'Do you do a lot of island travelling?'

'Yes. I'm addicted to it.'

'Where is it this time?'

'St Kilda.'

'Oh God! You *are* addicted. Black or white?'

'Black, please.'

'Yes, I thought it would be.'

The coffee steamed, the sun lit a flare path on the Minch, and I was back in Rum. That island's human story has been harrowing even by Hebridean standards. Famine, mass emigration, landlords infamous almost without exception for various forms of villainy or grandiose self-indulgence. One of all too recent memory was so relentless in pursuit of privacy that Rum became known as 'the Forbidden Isle'. Not that that stopped covert expeditions from trying.

Then there is Kinloch Castle, a monument to the Bullough family which sunk colossal wealth and ego and acquisitive greed into its monstrousness. It is a building without a redeeming feature, but when the island finally came into the possession of the then Nature Conservancy Council, the intact preservation of castle and contents was part of the deal. Whatever you think of the idea of an island going into public ownership, it is difficult to see a shred of justification for investing a penny of public money in the preservation of such a loathsome edifice as Kinloch Castle. It perpetuates only the memory of the worst kind of island lairds. In any setting the building would be a trial on the sensibilities of those who like a building to honour its sense of place. On Rum, it is a hideous affront, but nothing that a good fire and subsequent demolition couldn't rectify.

Rum continues to live an uneasy existence. Ownership has transferred from the NCC to its successor, Scottish Natural Heritage, which continues to manage it as a national nature reserve. Its geology is intriguing, its mountain-dwelling manx shearwater colony is a phenomenon, a long-term study of red deer is a remarkable project, as is an attempt to re-create something like a natural tree cover. Sea eagles have been reared there and released into the wild. There is talk of reintroducing wolves. There is no talk of rebuilding human life there, and the present small population is mostly at the beck and call of SNH. Perhaps the past carries too strong a taint for Rum to flourish again, but it is not a healthy precedent to establish which segregates high-profile nature conservation and a land-using human population. We need both in equipoise if the seaboard islands of Scotland are to turn that old, old tide which has drained so much of the lifeblood from them.

Yet from a distance, it is such an enticing prospect. Seton Gordon once wrote of the Rum mountains (in that half-Gaelic lilt which characterised his English): 'Very pleasant did those island hills appear in the soft evening sunlight . . . Slowly the glow deepened on Rum; slowly the glory on its hills faded . . .' There is much about Rum's old glories which has faded. Seton Gordon was on Canna at the time, enchanted by distance. From there it is easier to turn a blind eye on the glory that *was* Rum. Unleash the wolf there by all means and let it be free there. It has been a long, long time since anything so wise and compassionate and tolerant as a wolf was top dog on Rum.

'Very pleasant did those island hills appear in the soft evening
sunlight,' wrote Seton Gordon, 'slowly the glow deepened on
Rum; slowly the glory faded . . .'

The following spring I was on Eigg, sailing out of Glen Uig, an eye on Rum as usual. This time it was hot, and a dark blueness went almost uniformly through sea and mountains and sky as though nature had tired of the old scheme of things and colour-washed the whole lot with a view to starting again. Very pleasant did those island hills appear across their expanse of sea. At Eigg, a curious ritual was performed. We passengers disembarked, a small knot of islanders boarded, the boat stood off a few lengths from the shore, and thus out of the land's jurisdiction it became a bar for the islanders. Eigg has no pub.

Eigg bewitched me. You can only be bewitched by Eigg if you are a visitor, only enjoy idyllic days if you are taking your ease, if you do not live there. Such are the troubled dealings between islander and landowner, but Eigg is hardly unique in that respect. In fact all the Small Isles seem plagued by it. Canna was the exception under the benevolent regime of John Lorne Campbell, but he handed over to the National Trust for Scotland and it has fared less well for the islanders from that point on.

As I write, Keith Schellenberg, laird of Eigg, has announced he will sell the island. The way he put it, in a strongly worded newspaper interview, he had had enough. The struggle was unequal. The islanders were 'barmy'.

Eigg in rare oceanic calm as islanders contemplate a new future embracing both crofting and wildlife conservation

The last straw had been a fire which had destroyed his vintage Rolls-Royce. The islanders were looking longingly towards Assynt where a year or two earlier crofters had bought the estate and warmed hearts the length of the West Highland seaboard. Neither laird nor islander was about to shed a tear over the parting of the ways on Eigg, but the island mood was for change, for a better way of doing things which embraced both crofting and wildlife conservation. Perhaps that old, old tide can be turned yet.

Too many small islands change hands too often for the wrong reasons. The estate agents' advertisements will detail the number of stags, the prospects for the grouse and the fishing, but not the human population. No one tells you that you are buying not just the island but also someone else's way of life, not just their present but their future as well, and their past which is dear to them and locked deep inside and kept from your incomer's eyes.

Our islands are rich because of the infinite variations of wild nature there and because of the way of life which is rooted in tradition, inheritance, and continuity. It should be an offence to deny or corrupt or diminish that richness, but it is not.

I had idyllic days on Eigg. The weather held, I walked endlessly, watched otters, and in a May heatwave I climbed the Sgurr of Eigg which is among the foremost of all island rocks. It is not just the summit of the island. It also defines its island from limitless sea, island and West Highland miles away. I climbed softly across the summit rocks for the place is one of those high rock outposts which imparts something like a sense of sanctity. There I surprised a golden eagle, sunning drowsily on a ledge below the summit. She was a huge female, and she simply stepped off the rock with her wings wide. She was ten yards away when she lifted off and her wings filled the world. When I finally lost sight of her against the distant landmass of Ardnamurchan she was the size of a sparrow and her wings had not so much as rippled, not once. There, I told myself, is the true laird of the Hebrides.

The blue weather held, and on the way back to Glenuig the boat stopped at Rum long enough for me to canter up among the rocks to redress something of the imbalance with which Rum had lodged in my mind. That evening I watched Rum and Eigg blacken against a band of pale gray which lay like a low wall on the horizon. Above and below the wall were the fire shades of sunset. Too often that is the way of it – the full potential of the islands walled in while the natural world blazes around them . . .

The steward was back for the empty coffee cup, the plane was preparing to land on a piece of rolled-out pastry lying flat on the Atlantic. Its name was Benbecula.

'St Kilda? Rather you than me, Sir. Good luck.'

I smiled, wishing he hadn't said that.

In the terminal building I tried to look helpless, confident that someone would be there to point me in the right direction. I couldn't be hard to recognise. I was the passenger with the typewriter. No one advanced from the throng. Gaelic greetings cut conspicuously through the hubbub.

I saw a man in Army uniform holding a large sign. It said: 'St Kilda passengers'. I introduced myself. I was on his list. Good. He ticked me off, then asked for my 'whereabouts between now and 18.00 hours'.

The Army base on St Kilda is the only permanent occupation there. They look after the radar station on one of the hilltops. I was to sail with the Army in their flat-bottomed landing craft, the island's main supply line. She was a notorious craft, a notoriously eccentric crosser of the forty miles of open ocean. As one veteran confided in me, 'She wallows like a drunken pig, that bitch.'

I considered the soldier's question. The short answer was that I hadn't a clue. What does everyone else do? I asked.

'Gowdennadahkoilan,' he said.

Not Gaelic, anyway.

'Sorry?'

'They gowdennadahkoilan.'

'Denna . . . I'm sorry, I don't know what you mean.'

'The Dahk Oiland Owtel.'

I went in search of elucidation. I guessed I was looking for the Dark Island Hotel. I asked an airport official where it was.

'Four or five miles. You'll get a taxi outside.'

Outside there was a Range Rover and a tractor and trailer. Neither looked like taxis. I tried again with the same official. A man with whom he had been talking interrupted:

'Not at all. I'll give you a lift.'

'That's very kind. Are you sure it's not out of your way?'

'Actually, yes it is, but what else am I going to do this morning?'

He was a Benbecula man, all his life, he said as we drove. I put his life at about seventy years thus far. He waved to every single vehicle and human we passed, every one. By way of conversation I invoked the name of the only Benbecula native I'd ever encountered, a man long domiciled on the lower half of the mainland. He frowned and nodded.

'Oh yes,' he said at once. 'He's got wife trouble, hasn't he?'

I whiled away the long warm afternoon on Benbecula's miles of empty white and pink and green beaches . . . white sand, pink mats of thrift, green machair. Wader birds crammed the shore. Bonxies cruised among the gulls,

'I whiled away the long warm afternoon on Benbecula's miles of empty white and pink and green beaches . . . white sand, pink mats of thrift, green machair'

'A voice gatecrashed a dream: "Anybody want to see St Kilda?
It's worth a look" '

looking menacing. Mind you, a bonxie looks menacing when it's having a bath or sunbathing. An otter showed briefly on a rock, an old, gray-grizzled beast with a wounded leg, but he dived again as soon as he saw me. Moments later he was a hundred yards out, lying on his back and eating contentedly at a twitching fish.

I used the afternoon to try and settle myself. The drive from home to Glasgow Airport, the flight, Stevenson, Rum, the airport confusion, the drive dennadahkoilan . . . it had all made chaotic inroads into my state of mind. I was going to camp alone for two weeks on St Kilda and between my destination and me lay what I had been assured was the appalling prospect of the sail on the drunken pig.

She looked well enough alongside at Lochboisdale in South Uist. My trepidation abated a touch when a new acquaintance I had made dennadahkoilan turned out to be someone big in the construction company building something new on St Kilda's radar station. He whisked me up aloft to the officers' mess and saw to it that I was treated regally. Hours later, well out into the Atlantic, the drunken pig was demure and sober and gently soporific. I slept on a benign ocean.

A voice gatecrashed a dream.

'Anybody want to see St Kilda? It's worth a look.'

Chapter Six

NATURE'S LAST LIMIT

MY WATCH SAID 5 a.m. I went up on deck and saw St Kilda. It was purple and it was worth a look. It was a cardboard cut-out wedged upright between the waves, and it was purple. I had never seen a purple island before.

Then I saw the other St Kildas, paler shades scattered further off, and I began, slowly, to realise that the first glance had revealed the least of it. What turned out to be the dour outrider of Levenish was suddenly framed not by a misted northern sky but by perhaps the most audacious thing in nature I have ever seen, an inconceivable island shape, a petrified sea monster heaved more than 1,200 feet up out of the ocean – Boreray. Not just Boreray, either, but also Stac Lee, a mere 600 feet high but quite high enough for any lopsided parallelogram with no visible means of support.

Weeks of map-poring helped to make sense of the materialising shapes, but distance and vertical scale confounded understanding. Our approach from the south (not the east as I had anticipated) threw Levenish against Boreray so I mistook Boreray for Hirta, the main island. Then the boat dipped and I realised bits of superstructure were concealing the view. I ran to the bow where wider miles of ocean lay unobscured, and there was Hirta with Dùn, its eccentric breakwater seemingly folded against it. Every impact was vertical, but so fragmented and so scattered the fragments that it was not possible to take it all in at once.

But these first moments became my definition of St Kilda, the one I have carried in my mind ever since. I see the place in the dawn. I see the north sky navy blue and smoored, I see it pale to lilac, then smother itself in herring-bones of flimsy clouds which began to vanish almost as they formed. I remember an ocean almost flat. I remember that so mysterious and two-dimensional were the island shapes, so aloof in their distance and their

'I considered myself the luckiest mortal afloat and prepared for
Village Bay. It was 7 a.m. . . .'

*St Kilda's isolation and capacity for brewing mists have fooled
many aircraft pilots . . . the islands are scattered with wrecks*

dawn that I might have been the first of all St Kilda's voyagers, nomadic herdsmen coming curiously up the margins of Europe. This, they would conclude, must be nature's last limit, for they would be accustomed to sail only to land which was within sight. On St Kilda, the only land which is (very occasionally) in sight is the land you have left behind to get here.

Perhaps, having got this far, they would contemplate dismally St Kilda's armour of cliffs and wonder if there was so much as a scrap of fertility or shelter. They would have the sense of Village Bay long before they rounded the south-east tip of Dùn and saw its mile-wide embrace. They would see that the shelf of almost level ground around its northmost curve was immune to all storms save a south-easterly. (Some things have not changed on St Kilda. Today's mariner has the same choice when a south-easterly blows: he must run before it round the island to north-facing Loch a' Ghlinne and sit it out there. Nature still sets the rules.)

St Kilda advanced and bore down hugely on the drunken pig, which, to be fair, had proved as stable as Boreray. I considered myself the luckiest mortal afloat and prepared for Village Bay. It was 7 a.m. and the sun was strong and warm.

After such an unfurling of islands, Village Bay was too anti-climactic for comfort. There were the backdrop hills familiar from a thousand photographs, there was the old village street in its neat and half-derelict crescent. There was the Army camp, quite the ugliest infliction of bad buildings on a supreme landscape that I have ever seen. There were the hilltop radar masts. There was the road which connected hilltop to shore. There was the wondrous whittle-work of Dùn's long ridge, 600 feet high and a mile long and skinny and precipitous and fissured as a bar of Toblerone. (The teeth which gnaw at it are the sea's: already it has bitten through the Dùn Passage where once there was a land bridge to Hirta; habitually a roaring south-westerly creams into a groove on its seaward flank and hurdles the ridge, all 600 feet of it, to fall in Village Bay, salt rain.) You can look at the staggering, multiform scope of that St Kildan curve which surrounds Village Bay and you can argue that it is a small portion of it all which the Army presence besmirches, nothing more than a footnote to that rearing vertical scale which Conachair imposes on Hirta. Yet St Kilda is a World Heritage Site, the only one we have in Scotland. The citation, the work of the World Heritage Convention of UNESCO, 1987, reads:

> Through the collective recognition of the community of nations expressed within the principles of the convention concerning protection of the world cultural and natural heritage, the St Kilda Archipelago of the National Trust for Scotland has been designated a World Heritage

Site and joins a select list of protected areas around the world whose outstanding natural and cultural resources form the common inheritance of all mankind.

But what is the worth of such a designation if it does not preclude something as vile as the Army's power station, a building which would look offensive on a derelict industrial estate in Birmingham. On St Kilda it is an affront. No, it is not the scale of the besmirching which offends. It is that there is besmirching at all.

The drunken pig 'docked' in Village Bay by pointing itself at a concrete slipway and – very slowly and carefully – crashing into it. It is a good metaphor for a technique much used by the Army on St Kilda. But one way or another, things have been crashing into St Kilda for a very, very long time . . . the sea tirelessly reshaping the place; the weather which has had an entire ocean to work up a head of steam by the time it gets here; and mankind, which for 4,000 years has claimed the place for his common inheritance . . . his boats of every shape and sophistication. His tourism when he finally got round to inventing it was one of the most damaging crash-landings of all. Even his aircraft have scattered the islands with wreckages and put their small scars on the landscape.

Yet curiously, the simple civilisation which humankind evolved on St Kilda only ever dignified the place. It seemed to have acknowledged from the outset that the only way to live in such a place, such an out-station of nature, was by nature's rules, by honouring a sense of place as a first commandment. When you think about it, nothing else makes much sense. On St Kilda, throughout all its eras before the wretched Victorians started turning up in steamerfuls to gawp at what they saw as a primitive human zoo, all that was available to the islander was all that was available in the islands. They had seabirds and sheep for food and clothing, stone and turf for building, and they lived peaceably and well, without crime.

It seems strange to go to such a landscape as St Kilda and be moved by people. There are people everywhere, after all, yet there is nothing else like St Kilda. While I was there I shared a few momentous hours with the crew of a small yacht out among Boreray and the stacs. Among the crew was a Mull man, a seaman all his life and on all the world's seas. It was his thirtieth trip to St Kilda. He had seen nothing like it in the world, he said, although he had heard of good things among the offshore islands of New Zealand which he had not seen. To me, St Kilda emerged in its dawn as though through the eyes of someone else, someone far, far back. Inevitably, the practicalities and the landscape wounds intervened but the thread of that idea never left me. Each time I turned my back on Village Bay and crossed the watershed into Gleann Mor – there especially – I felt the old eyes again. The topography of St Kilda is such that it demands introspection. Nothing in the limitless miles of sea commands the way St Kilda does. St Kilda from the sea is a startling sensation. St Kilda from St Kilda breaks every rule of landscape watching which I have ever invented for myself. The closer you get to it, the better it gets.

I was lucky. I was able to walk alone and more or less as I pleased as long as I told the Nature Conservancy Council wardens where I was going and carried the distress flare they gave me and avoided one or two particularly sensitive wildlife places (the peregrine cliffs, the bonxies' bathing pool, for example). The few island shapes of St Kilda quickly became familiar and the old eyes demanded that I look deeper.

I made all the excursions the first-time traveller to St Kilda does, but over and over again, I crossed into Gleann Mor, over the 800-foot watershed of Mullach Sgar which bisects Hirta into its two habitable worlds. It is a wide, green place, Gleann Mor, or at least by St Kildan standards it is. The oldest evidence of human settlement is here, not in the more reliable shelter of Village Bay. The old eyes suggest two good reasons.

One is that they were pastoral nomads, and Gleann Mor is what passes for pasture here. (For as long as St Kildans kept cattle, long after Village Bay became the centre of population, cattle were pastured in Gleann Mor; there were even shielings and the island women crossed Mullach Sgar twice a day carrying milk in buckets suspended on a shoulder harness.) Their beasts would be their priority. They would live where their beasts could thrive. They would thrive best in Gleann Mor.

The old eyes suggest a second, more audacious, possibility. It is one I found easy to accommodate, because it is a doctrine I subscribe to, a natural spirituality, a religion founded on landscape. It is that these nomads, questing the rim of the continent 4,000 years ago, feeling their way up the seas of the planet, were moved, perhaps even led, by the power of landscape. The Western Isles would have been exquisite enough then, not so much as a MacBrayne's steamer to cross your bow. But a glimpse of St Kilda against a sunset from such as Loch Druidibeg on South Uist, a staunch splendour of isolation, would be a pilgrimage no disciple of landscapes could resist. Likewise, it would be the beauty of Gleann Mor (and it is a bright place for all its hemming walls and north-facing tendencies) which would outweigh the practicalities of Village Bay. You do not *settle* on St Kilda if your mind is run by practicalities.

It was the old eyes, too, which accompanied me to the summit of Conachair, the summit of all Hirta (the memorable statistic of 1,234 feet), but outreached by Soay (1,239 feet) and Boreray (1,259 feet). I made three ascents. On the first two the world was rimmed by curtains of mist and skittish storms, and I felt for the first time the awesome sense which accompanies the realisation that there is no land in any direction as you turn through 360 degrees, none other than this St Kilda where you stand. The third ascent drew back the curtains, the sea was its richest shade of blue which was not quite navy, and the Western Isles were visible, dark shapes low to the water as shipwrecks, laced with their miles of white sands which showed as fine threads.

The old eyes made these responses to Conachair's revelations: to the land-less view they raised St Kilda's status higher up out of the ocean, raised the marvel of the place, turned my eyes inward looking deeper; to the rare revelation – a handful of days a year – of the Western Isles, the old eyes raised one great convulsive shrug, not relief but indifference. At that moment I knew that my eyes had begun to reach below St Kilda's surface. The first layer of the first imprint of the first scratch, the first awareness of the power of introspection in such a landscape. I sensed it first on a summit, but I would sense it deepest in Gleann Mor.

I walked across the top of the island and descended the steeps into Gleann Mor where those first settlers decided to dare to call St Kilda home. All over the glen and even high on its wind-shredded western rim lies the fractured skeleton of their eras, fragments of souvenirs com-memorating the day they set stone on stone, however they set it, whenever the day might have been. It was a skill the St Kildans never lost until the day the last of them stooped under their own lintel, that dark day of 1930, when at their own request, the few remaining St Kildans were evacuated. When you see a bad building on St Kilda you know it post-dates the St Kildans.

I walked the glen, putting names to the orchids and the wetland flowers, bowing respectfully or ducking ungraciously before the hair-parting bonxies, scanning the bathing pool for ornithology's fly-by-nights. St Kilda is the kind of oceanic pause on the flightpaths of the world's birds where almost anything can turn up: in my two weeks here I saw snow bunting, phalarope, velvet scoter and golden eagle, in addition to the teeming seabird regimes which overwhelm every St Kildan day outwith the long, gray winter. The pool lies low in the glen, not far above the small cliff where waterfalls clatter into the sea. It is the only fresh-water sheet of any description in all St Kilda. The bonxies guard it diligently, and they are persuasive guards. Having bathed, they retire to nearby knolls to stand and dry off. They are big and dark and muscly and suitably impressive. They turn puffins inside out for a living.

Feel the width of the glen, cool in the wind that hurries down from the watershed and fans out round the walls. You can almost see it roll downhill, like a mist or a glacier. What faces first lifted to that wind, cool in which hot summer? What ears attuned to its high song among the boulders of Mullach Mor, the crags of Mullach Bi?

Feel the width of the wind. Was it that width which endeared the early St Kildans to Gleann Mor? There is little enough of width in that loose knot of islands, little enough of spaciousness. There are days in Village Bay with the cloud camped 500 feet above your head and the world curtained to a single seaward mile when you feel as if the great bulk of Conachair and Oiseval have devised a conspiracy to edge you off the island altogether, so close and dark their slopes have grown. On such a day, too, I would cross instinctively into Gleann Mor, cleaving through the cloud on the watershed, and find solace in the green spread which lay beneath the clouds. I could never get enough of Gleann Mor.

I used to sit and scan every shelf and non-shelf from the low ground to the high rim, every scrap of ground which looked to my eye to be capable of holding a shieling or some other small building. Every one I chose had been built on, but so were countless others where I wouldn't have given a prayer for their chances of surviving, far less offer comfort and shelter. Then there were the nonsenses, where I fancied one stone set on another wouldn't last an hour, never mind an eon, yet there they still stand, or there at least something of them still stands. The large-scale map indicates 'Hut Circle' high on the south-west corner of the glen. But high on the south-west corner of the glen also means high on the cliffs of Mullach Bi, for like all St Kilda's hillsides, the west slopes of Gleann Mor are one-sided. Their 'other side' is a 1,000-foot sea cliff, and it is there on a blunt knife-edge between glen and sea and a thousand feet up in the air that one of St Kilda's civilisations saw fit to build a hut circle.

Its purpose may have been strategic, for nearby is the name Claigeann na Tigh Faire. Claigeann means 'skull' and may just refer to the small, bald clifftop path where the Tigh Faire, the watch-house, stood. It's an unchancy place for a building, whatever the motive, for there is arguably no more storm-brutalised shore in Europe than that one.

And what about that cleit on the seaward side of the uncompromising headland of the Cambir – is that twentieth century? Fifteenth? Tenth? Lean on it if you dare. The cliff trembles and gives way, becomes a cave. The cave caves in, becomes a stac. The cleit, though, built by man from the stuff of nature, ordering it to give it added strength, still stands. It is rare to find man taking nature's raw material and improving on its natural purpose with his own skills. Now and again on St Kilda it happened and you find the evidence and you wonder how many years after the event you found it. It is one of the reasons why you come to such a landscape as St Kilda and find yourself moved by people.

Their most extraordinary intact structure, however, is back over the watershed, in the lap of Conachair above Village Bay. There, on a rough and boggy slope, lie four stone-walled enclosures for crops or sheep or both. They are sprawling things, pale-stoned, fashioned from the hillside boulders and following no known geometric plan. One of them is split into four, each section as shapeless as the next, governed no doubt by the lie of the land and whether or not there was an unmovable rock in the path of any chosen line. I loved them for their spur-of-the-moment logic. The orderly curve and regular spaces and proportions of the street in Village Bay are not the fruits of St Kildan minds, but rather a nineteenth-century replacement street urged on the St Kildans by the minister of the day. No one can deny that his plan and the simplicity of the buildings honour their sense of place well enough, but look at their ordered regime then come up to An Lag Bho'n Tuath and read the minds of the St Kildans at work – read them in the stones.

The original purpose of my trip here was a different book, a collaboration with photographer Colin Baxter published by his own company in 1988, *St Kilda – A Portrait of Britain's Remotest Island Landscape*. The poem 'Sheep Folds: An Lag Bho'n Tuath' was first published in that book:

Whose geometries were these,
whose manhandling eye
accorded every stone its place
and every line its uncouth rhyme
an unrefined stone poem?

These frames of mind
uncluttered by rigidities
of round and square
made rude amends
by hoarding stones the size
of shepherds to their bidding,
and these, worked well, land-sure,
were true enough.

The four sheep folds
stand sheepless now
but gathered by

their shepherding hills
they tend their careful flock
of teeming stones.

Such men who wrought
such shapes upon the land
are sorely missed: St Kilda
craves again the rock-sure clasp
of such ungeometric hands.

There are many small miracles of building on St Kilda, stone masonry rather than architecture, instinctive solutions to practical difficulties. But I doubt if, in the modern era at least, they ever built anything better than the enclosures of An Lag.

The St Kildans' most extraordinary structure lies in the lap of
Conachair ... stone-walled enclosures fashioned from the hillside
boulders and following no known geometric plan ...

*'The Tunnel is landscape out of the top drawer ... you find framed
in that mighty rock yawn the surreal offshore spectacle of Boreray'*

Back in Gleann Mor, nature was lining up a masterpiece of its own. Loch a' Ghlinne is a bite of ocean deep into Hirta's north coast, bounded by headlands. The Cambir to the west dips then climbs to a heady stance 600 feet above the ocean. To the east is the Gob na h-Airde, unprepossessing as St Kilda headlands go and reached by way of that rarest of St Kilda landscapes, a piece of level ground. It is not much of a piece of level ground, more a narrow pause between contours, but at its northern end, concealed to all but the most prying of eyes, there is a rock ramp which limpets down the cliff face among razorbills and guillemots. When, hours later, you squirm back up the ramp, your life will have been changed.

The level ground is called Leacan an t-Sluic Mhóir. It is another of those Gaelic phrases which is best swallowed whole in the language which spawned it, for the translation loses everything. But for what it is worth, *leacan* is flagstones, *sluic* is a hole, and you end up with 'the flagstones of the big hole'. What you get on the ground is a level clifftop terrace of bare rock which leads to a big hole such as you have never seen, nature's ultimate St Kildan phenomenon – the Tunnel.

Old St Kilda regulars (once you have announced, however casually, your intention to go they emerge from the woodwork bombarding you with advice and cautionary tales) warn you about the Tunnel. They sing its praises and blow its trumpet, and heap its name with such superlatives that you approach with trepidation: what if you are unimpressed? Mostly though, the trumpet-blowers played the thing down, for memory in such a landscape is not to be trusted. The Tunnel is landscape out of the top drawer, and made the more memorable because you can stand on its roof and not know it's there.

Imagine an aircraft hangar, the kind they used to keep Lancaster bombers in half a dozen at a time. Its roof and walls are solid rock and, say, 200 feet thick. Its floor is also rock, sloping steeply down towards a great trench which runs through the middle of the hangar from front to back. Both ends are open, and at both ends, the sea comes in.

It doesn't just 'come' in, though, it thunders. And when it is halfway through, still thundering, it meets the other sea coming the other way. All this throws up its monstrous voice into an echo chamber the size of a headland. *That* is the Tunnel, but don't take my word for it. I can tell you are unconvinced.

Seals come in with the sea, for no good reason that I can think of other than to be where two seas meet. Watch them dive down the inestimable depths, see them climb up and up back to the surface of the underworld. There are no cleaner, clearer seas than these fragments of the Atlantic where they meet head-on. Watching the seals in their boisterous strip of ocean, you get a glimpse of an inkling of the unseen depths through which an island like this anchors itself to the rest of the planet.

One sound detached itself from the cacophony of echo, one pure thread of song, familiar yet rendered unfamiliar by the volume of amplification offered by that gaunt auditorium. In any other setting that pert songster is a small sound, one of nature's grace notes. In the Tunnel it grew to something symphonic, a throbbing fluency of music which sprang from its own well on a high ledge among the rafters of the Tunnel. It was a St Kilda wren, and it sang unstoppably.

The wren is the charmer of St Kilda, confident in its celebrity status, for it is its own sub-species, bigger (by wren standards, that is) and sweeter-voiced than its mainland kin. The Tunnel is all in nature that the cathedral is in man. It is huge and cool and dim within. The light from its vast glass-less and unstained windows blazes beyond its walls but diffuses and dwindles within. The vaulted roof is the same mystery of the sculptor's art. There is the same spirit of sanctity born of high endeavour and grand gesture and ancient stones. In the cathedral of the Tunnel, the wren is the choirboy, antheming nature.

Finally, when you think the Tunnel has thrown its entire stockpile of sensation at you, you slither down towards the sea at its eastern entrance and find framed in that mighty rock yawn the surreal offshore spectacle of Boreray.

Boreray never just appears. It always has to make an entrance, the star, the showstopper island of the group. Now it reared up out of its ocean, characteristically monstrous. You almost expect it to roar, to feel the Tunnel shudder as it tries to contain such an unstoppable image. But when Boreray materialises in the mouth of the Tunnel, it has encountered the one thunder it cannot steal. The Tunnel is the sea's great endeavour here. Boreray is the land's. But land and sea both know that one of St Kilda's eras will eventually dawn when Boreray will be smooth on the ocean floor and the sea will roll on alone above to be smitten by sun and storm where Boreray once ruled.

The two most turbulent, troubling and tumultuous scraps of Scotland's western seaboard, one framed by the other, but the framing only possible because Boreray is four miles distant, grand gesture within grand gesture, cathedral within cathedral . . .

. . . You retrace your steps through the Tunnel, back up the ramp, out into the overworld, out on to the Flagstones of the Big Hole where you sit in the sun with your mind numb.

How do you follow that?

Where do you go? It is too soon to cross the watershed again and hem yourself in to the village. So where?

There is a place . . .

The walk around the shore of Loch a' Ghlinne is a slow antidote. This being St Kilda, you do not walk the shore of course, but the clifftop edge anything between 100 and 600 feet above the shore. The descent to the shore is for waterfalls and fulmars and hanging columns of sea campion, rose root and other botanical eccentrics which thrive in such headlong places. Botanists also descend here, to marvel. And a day dawned, 4,000 years ago, when a handful of cautious, shadowy seamen stepped ashore and manhandled reluctant, nervous beasts ashore, up over these same flowering rocks.

It is a steep and tortuous haul back from the shore up on to the tilting headland of the Cambir, skirting the cliff which cornices the high wall of Gleann Mor to the west. That north-west thrust of Hirta rollicks northwards from the 1,000-foot contour in a series of switchbacking swoops to a narrow neck 600 feet lower. Disconcertingly, the ocean never seems to get any nearer, despite the long, windswept descent. Halfway down, the map intones 'Settlement' in that Gothic script it uses to denote antiquity. You pause and look at where you are, and there is not a more exposed and unsettlement-like spot on earth. You shake your head and charge on down.

At its lowest, narrowest point, the headland chicanes and begins to widen and steepen again, until finally you stand on a small apex and the sea is 650 feet below your feet. This is the Cambir. Here, over a long, late and dawdling lunch, and slowly, as your mind churns sluggishly back into some kind of functioning order, you can begin to put something of St Kilda into some kind of perspective.

I love this kind of airy pedestal in any landscape, especially when it occupies the middle ground of the airspace – higher than the immediate surroundings, the land from which it springs, but deferring to greater heights from a respectful distance. Standing on the Cambir you are high enough above Loch a' Ghlinne to feel a kind of overlordship, such as you are unaware of, for example, when you walk the Flagstones of the Big Hole. The Tunnel's headland is lowly from here, the mouth of the Tunnel nothing more than the mouth of one more cave. Loch a' Ghlinne has many mouths. But Conachair is a mighty upthrust, and that 1,200-foot curtain of cliff which it drapes sheer to the sea is dark and mesmerising, a stupendous fall.

PREVIOUS PAGE: *'I had grown as detached from St Kilda as any evacuated St Kildan'*

And there is Boreray, of course, unframed now but drenched in cloud. The gannet-white wedge of Stac Lee looks as if it has been embedded in Boreray's flank from here, a trick of sightlines, for just like Ramna Stacs in far Shetland, Boreray and its two acolytes are forever shuffling about the ocean and changing shape.

Something like a mountain range has been amassing at your back to the south while you have walked north to the Cambir. It is not a mountain range, of course, because all St Kilda's summits are illusory, clifftops not hilltops. But the rock upthrusts of Mullach Bi and Claigeann Mor, Ruival and Dùn have aligned and foreshortened Hirta's western seaboard into a fair impersonation of the Cuillin Ridge. Distance deceives too. Dùn is four miles away from here, and Boreray five sea miles. It is a bigger place than you thought. Lonely, unsung Levenish is five miles away to the south-east, the same distance as Stac Lee in the north-east, and the two stacs are almost six miles apart.

Then you turn again, and a new St Kildan world is at your feet and above your level gaze: the wide, blunt arrowhead of Soay, and the stuttering fragments of the land bridge which once attached it to Hirta. Soay Stac and Stac Biorach are the remains, the summit ridge of underwater Cuillin. Soay Stac is the more intact of the two, but withering fast. The sea has already worked an arch clear through its skinny wall; how long before the map must be drawn to show 'Soay Stacs'? Stac Biorach is 'the sharp-pointed stac' which may have been true once (and it does have a needle-ish aspect from the sea) but its crown has been worn down into a sheltering dish which the guillemots and kittiwakes have not been slow to colonise. Together they are the shaky stepping-stones for a confident giant (perhaps the Amazon who reputedly once inhabited Gleann Mor, the spot still enigmatically marked on the map as 'Amazon's House') to cross the quarter mile of ocean which wallows flatulently between Soay and Hirta.

Soay is a lost place, a small, green and sloping plateau atop a forbidding stockade of dark, leaning cliffs. Not even the St Kildans, matchless cliff-climbers that they were, went eagerly on to Soay. Landing requires a flat calm or a helicopter. The St Kildans had few enough of the former and the latter was still hovering over the drawing-board when they evacuated. There are cleits on Boreray. There are none on Soay. There is a small and self-sufficient flock of sheep, and there are the birds. Probably a wren sings on some implausible pinnacle.

It grew warm in the late afternoon, the wind faltering, the Cambir the most delectable bit of rock on the planet. I sat on and on, the sun high and the sea slack. On that lofty belvedere drenched in that sun, I tried to revisit the Tunnel in my mind.

'From Oiseval, Dun is a black wedge tilted violently away from the bay. As often as not, the only visible shade of colour was in the sky behind it . . .'

It is an old trick I first began to use in the Cairngorms, sitting on high summer's plateau and trying to conjure up the midwinter mountain, ice-bloated grasses at my feet under a vast frost-haloed moon, the mountain not summer green but the blue-white of ghosts. The purpose of such conscious daydreaming is to seek out a closer bond with the landscape. The method is to fuse two of the landscape's extremes into a single pure strand of thought. That way, whenever the landscape is recalled or revisited, I see not the surface of the land under one particular set of circumstances, but something bonded and deeper.

What deepens is understanding of that creature of nature which is the landscape. It is like watching a migrant bird, say a whooper swan which winters in Britain. However much you watch it, you begin to understand the total bird only when you have also watched it in its Icelandic breeding grounds. When you go there to watch it, you must take with you the familiarity of the winter bird you know (ice-footed on the edge of a frozen Highland lochan) and create in your own mind a single creature from those two extremes of its workaday life.

The landscape also knows such extremes, although it is rare enough to

Bonxie . . . the old eyes of Gleann Mor

encounter two in a single day. The point of dwelling on them so consciously is simply to walk closer with nature, but it is hard work, and elusive as St Kildan flat calms.

The sun beat down on the Cambir, and 600 feet above the ocean the wind finally dropped. For an hour that oceanic fingerpost grew hot and still, an aloof fragment of St Kilda poised halfway between the sea and the islands' summits, and somehow not really belonging to either realm. In that unreal hour I pushed my mind back down the island. I saw the sun ignite a small flock of kittiwakes against the black mouth of the Tunnel, saw them dive down inside. In my mind I went with them. I was that outrider bird on the right wing of the flock, cleaving the warm air, the unaccustomed heat on my back and stiffly held gliding wings. It would be cooler down near the sea.

The flock's entry into the Tunnel was utterly different from the way I had gone in. I had crept, tentative on wet rock, in awe of the place. The kittiwakes gatecrashed its sanctity, raucous and confident, even when the sun on their backs switched off and the world grew dim and cathedral-cool.

I tried to contrive an image of the Tunnel, not from my own careful crouch on the sloping floor, but buoyantly cleaving the heart of its airspace amid the wavering of white, black-tipped wings and the reverberations of twenty quietly crying kittiwake throats. Then I tried to imagine myself back in my concealed crouch against the Tunnel wall as the kittiwakes came through. That would have silenced the wren! See how luminous the birds are in the gloom. Hear how the individual voices of the flock separate from each other in that spellbinding acoustic, so that you can put a voice to a particular bird, then that glorious moment when you open your throat as you glide, and your own voice spills, elemental as wind and spindrift, out into the cavern, up into its vaults, away and away on limitless echoes, sound's wings: 'Kitt-ay-wake . . . kitt-ay-wake . . .!'

To see St Kilda as the kittiwake sees it, that would be something.

But I was high on the Cambir and the wind was stirring, and with it the sea, whitening the base of Soay Stac again, and curving up over the small dorsal fin of Stac Dona, and putting a white stripe down its rock where a great fissure was opening. While I watched the sea stirring, I was thinking about the kittiwakes, and wondering why they would take to the Tunnel at all. They have always struck me as the airiest of seabirds. They like it best where the water is whitest, flying eagerly in the exhilaration of storms, relishing the charging air. Why take to the Tunnel, where I could envisage shags and cormorants, perhaps, furtive nesters that they are. But kittiwakes?

It occurred to me then that the moment – the only moment – that I had seen them enter the Tunnel was during that uncanny lull, that windlessness, that oceanic idleness. Where, in all St Kilda, would there be white water, a pool of turbulence in such a calm? Where else but in the heart of the Tunnel where the two seas collided!

I took the high road back to the tent, over Mullach Bi, Claigeann Mor, hugging the clifftop all the way to Ruaival which is the Cambir's counterpart in the south of the island. Ruaival, like all St Kilda's vantage points, has more than one compelling string to its bow. It sets the Village into its landscape (and also, alas, the Army camp) at the kind of distance which gives scope for your imagination to repopulate the long, green street and put a peat-reek on the air from rekindled hearths. But on such a day, when you have seen the cathedral and dawdled on the sun-bright brim of Hirta's most rarefied heights, the Village simply looks sad, as dour as Levenish, as lost as Soay.

Ruaival also overlooks the spindly ridge of Dùn, a loosely detached island with all Boreray's capacity to transform itself according to St Kilda's unending repertoire of lighting tricks. I remember it most fondly at dusk from the slopes of Oiseval above the tent. I made a small routine of my last waking moments each night I was on St Kilda of climbing up among Oiseval's boulderfields to a good flat rock and just sitting. Dùn from there is a black wedge tilted violently away from the bay. As often as not, the only visible shade of colour was in the sky behind it. The shape of Dùn would have been a massive presence in the St Kildans' lives. Whenever you lift your eye from the street it is there. If you happen to be walking the other way, facing Oiseval, you are more aware of Dùn at your back than Oiseval.

I was dawdling down the lower slopes of Ruaival when the young warden hailed me. There had been some discussion about arrangements for my homeward journey – I was in no rush, and dreading the moment – but now there was news that I could hitch a lift back to Mull on the two-masted schooner *Jean de la Lune* which I could see anchored in the bay. I knew the vessel by reputation (it had ferried my friend and collaborator Colin Baxter here and came highly recommended) and I took a snap decision to accept. She was leaving in two hours.

Striking camp quickly and without warning took the pain out of departure. Dave, the skipper, greeted me affably:

'Have you got any sea-sick pills?'

'Yes.'

'Well, start poppin 'em.'

When she sailed, I stood in the stern as St Kilda and I let each other go. The boat was full, but I stood alone. The passengers were a diving party and the overworld island was as indifferent to them as they were to it. I eavesdropped briefly on their conversation and envied them that underwater imagery of St Kilda which they knew of and I did not, for that too is part of the total island landscape and would be good to draw on.

The sea grew and grew that evening as St Kilda shrank back into its ocean womb. I was only sick once, briefly, when I made the serious misjudgment of trying to join the divers for a meal. One mouthful of curry was all it took to regurgitate lunch and breakfast too. I went back to the stern and stayed there till midnight, by which time it was almost dark and I had grown as detached from St Kilda as any evacuated St Kildan. I remembered Stevenson then, and no St Kildan would have been indifferent to his evocation of 'The Skye Boat Song' verse:

Billow and breeze
Islands and seas
Mountains of rain and sun;
All that was good,

All that was fair,
All that was me is gone.

There are only a handful of St Kildans left alive now. I met one a few months later. He was in his eighties and he had just been back, just once more. 'We all go back,' he said, 'just once more, as long as we are able.' I thought, how frail he looks, and how strong within. Like St Kilda.

On the *Jean de la Lune*, I wrote down four careful sentences without a pause, a rare occurrence in my writer's life. They appeared in my book *St Kilda* as the poem 'Soay at Dusk'. For some reason which escapes me now they had not been part of my original text for that book, but when Colin asked if I had a poem which might sit alongside his superb study of Soay blackly sunk under a lilac and purple sunset, I remembered the scrap of notebook paper. It accompanied Colin's photograph well enough, but it belonged truly to that last day on the boisterous deck of the *Jean de la Lune*. The paper is before me as I write, the words blurred from the spray of a breaking wave, the handwriting erratic from the motion of the craft.

And would the old stone-dwellers of Loch a' Ghlinne scale the Cambir to pilfer sunsets, store them in memory's cleits? Or had such suns no power to free minds so yolked to lands? And how many suns have Turnered Soay's amphitheatrical skies before and since, their exhibited art unscrutinised, their brushstrokes unremarked by the blinded eyes and turned backs of extinctions and evacuations? When our own momentary witness engraves one sky, one ocean, one island, with one sun's scribbling summer finger, we acknowledge suns which lit the volcanic birth and arced across the island's prime, until in its sea-crippled death throes, St Kilda prepared for 4,000 years of man.

The notebook is open on the desk. I read it with the old eyes of Gleann Mor.

Chapter Seven

THE ROAD TO ARNISH

EACH TIME I go to Raasay, I convince myself all over again that there is no more beautiful place in the land. I have been four times but I have passed the ferry slipway hundreds of times in pursuit of my Skye addiction. Each time I leave I vow to go more often, but four times in fifteen years is not often. The last time was a December day of fast squalls on a north wind and punctuations – commas and exclamation marks mostly – of sunshine between them. It was a combination which left me breathlessly questioning why I do not go more often to taste the single-malt beauty of Raasay.

The Skye addiction is part of the reason. It is always so good to be there, so eager am I for landscapes which have shaped half my life, friends whose faces fit the landscapes as readily as eagles. I pass the Raasay ferry as often as not with a fragment of Skye on my mind and a day's destination to fulfil. And even in the off-season the ferry fares are exorbitant. Raasay is an expensive luxury for the landscape watcher, an expensive necessity for the islander, but as with all single malts, you get what you pay for. Raasay is not just single malt. It is cask-strength landscape, mellow and fragrant and marvellous. Perhaps that is why it should not be rushed or overdone.

Raasay is four landscapes. Because of where it lies it offers unique insights into Skye and the mountains of Applecross, and the island itself is two islands. In the south it is limestone and almost fertile, and there are some good woods among the Forestry Commission plantations. Below the funnel of its famous landmark hilltop, Dun Caan, the rock falls in massive fissures down its mightily cliff-faced eastern shore. Here, under the fissures, eternally shadowed by the cliffs, is Hallaig. Here Sorley MacLean, native of this island, wrote his best-known and best-loved poem, the one which begins

Tha tìm, am fiadh, an coille Hallaig
Time, the deer, is in the wood of Hallaig

The north of Raasay is Torridonian sandstone. The woods are spartan birch, and it is all a different world. The two Raasays sustain two crofting communities, as different as their landscapes. In the north end, the crofters are go-ahead, innovative, industrious; in the south end they are traditional, reluctant to change or to labour, or so they say up at the north end.

So I was up at the north end and it was December and the snow was ripping the sky down in shreds on to the Sound of Raasay, then the wind would flap away the shreds and the Trotternish Ridge of Skye glittered and my breath was snatched away from me at every turn. I had a purpose of a kind at the north end, a small ambition, but one I had nurtured for quite a few years. I wanted to walk the road to Arnish, the one the whole of the West Highlands and the Hebrides knows as Calum's Road. If ever you wanted a symbol of the industriousness of the north-end crofter, or the umbilical nature of the attachment between the Gael and his land, you could do worse than walk the two miles of Calum's Road. It comes highly recommended by the writer and champion of Hebridean causes, Derek Cooper. In an added chapter to later editions of his admirable *Hebridean Connections*, he wrote:

> You should go to Raasay and walk Calum's Road and marvel at what he did. It holds out more hope for the future than all the reports ever written on the Highlands and Islands and all the speeches.

What Calum Macleod did with his road was build it. It had been forty years or so since the crofters of Arnish, Torran and South Rona had petitioned for a two-mile road to connect them with Brochel down the island a bit, where the road ended. The petition fell on deaf ears, and from a population of around a hundred, it whittled away down the years until there were just three. The school once taught between thirty and forty children. Now? You do not need a school for a township of ghosts.

Sorley MacLean wrote in *Hallaig*

> The window is nailed and boarded
> through which I saw the West

So in 1963, in addition to his duties as lighthousekeeper and crofter, Calum Macleod decided to build the road from his home at Arnish to Brochel. He would build it with his hands, and he would build it alone. It took him ten years and a now legendary toll on wheelbarrows, picks and spades. Authority was finally embarrassed into lending a hand – they did some of the dynamiting, and a couple of years after Calum finished it they tarmacked it. But Calum and his wife never owned a car, never drove on it. Tourists drive it of course, gingerly, for it's a tortuous route through a primeval landscape, never straight and never flat. Folk like me walk it both bemused and attracted by the bond between that islander and his island land. I marvel at its mute achievement. Calum was making a new stretch from the road end at Arnish to his cottage door when he died in 1988.

It is no meagre monument he has left.

The cairn stands on the high ground where his road began. They built it in 1990, two years after he died, honouring his unique labour of love of the land. It is a good Gaelic tradition, the building of a good cairn to mark its own kind, provided it *is* a good cairn, provided it stands well and does not defile where it stands. Calum Macleod was an exceptional worker of stone, as his road testifies. It was an inherited skill and he wielded it wonderfully. A bad cairn would not have done to mark his work. He has a good cairn.

I set off along his road into the teeth of the next snow squall, grimacing through my hood at my companion. If Andy Currie was cursing me fluently for inviting him out on such an escapade on such a day, he did so under his breath. I suspect, though, that he was enjoying the thing as much as I was. Andy is my great Skye friend, one time Nature Conservancy Council man on the ground for this part of the world. He has retired now, which is the NCC's loss (or Scottish Natural Heritage as they have now evolved). He was rare in that organisation in believing that the native island population should be as highly valued as the landscape and the wildlife. He made agreements which stuck because he believed in the people, in crofting, and because he won and never betrayed trust. He is the perfect companion for a trek in landscapes like these, as fond of the considerate silence as the thoughtful conversation. All along the island, from the ferry to Arnish and back, he was recognised and fondly greeted, and no one was troubled by the presence of a stranger like me on the island on such a December day.

The first thing you notice about Calum's Road is the way it fits the landscape, obeying contours. When you build by hand, you can do this.

The squall relented. Skye rushed out. From Ben Tianavaig by Portree all the way north to Staffin, the mighty crags of Trotternish – normally the blackest of Skye's landscape signatures – were white fires. Above them, jousting with the summits of Storr and Edra, cloudscapes the size of islands bore bleakly down, blurring the mountains' distinctions. The squall was forgotten, the discomfort of numbing fingers was shelved. If you want the

'Then the Trotternish Ridge of Skye glittered and my breath was
snatched away from me at every turn . . .'

*What Calum Macleod did with his road was build it. He built it
with his hands. He built it alone*

magic of the island midwinter you must take it in snatches and pay the price. The memory of it outlasts the discomfort by years. The retrospective value of such a day dwells on the snow spectacle, not the blue fingers. We were there when it happened. That is what matters.

The fragment of road which skirts Loch Arnish is its chief wonder. It is a blasted shelf above the sea. I thought of Calum Macleod going in alone among the blasted chaos, bottoming his road with pick and shovel and barrow and the stoical patience of the Gael in adversity. What was his frame of mind? Did he go each day with a missionary zeal? Was he just pig-headedly stubborn? Did he ever wish he had never started the thing . . . somewhere about here at the top of the hill above the hairpins, knowing the labour that lay ahead before he could begin to cut the road inland along the last historic half-mile? Every yard of that wretched contortion his road must follow round the corner of the loch would be visible, probably every working day for a couple of years. Did he rage at it, or did he go quietly back and forward, sure of his craft, convinced of the worth of the labour? Did he straighten in the dusk, admire the latest new yard, and like the anonymous, heroic cathedral stonemasons of Kirkwall 800 years before him, shoulder his tools and walk home through the evening, whistling quietly?

I would love to have known him, loved to have talked to him, because his was such a tangible and unsentimental expression of what it is the native islander brings to bear that stamps his race on his landscape, and permits his landscape to stamp his race.

Derek Cooper interviewed him in the 1970s for *Hebridean Connection*. A small glimmer of the man gleamed through a couple of sentences.

'There's no fear of you being run down by a car here or choked by dirty air or things like that,' he had said. 'And you have freedom. I always liked freedom.' Even the freedom to enslave yourself to the building of a road, it seems.

The croft land at Arnish was going back. The house stood empty after he died, too isolated for his widow to live alone. Rush grass and bracken needs no invitation to invade such a fertility as a piece of well-worked croft ground. The house looked trim enough, and two young men were going in about the place, moving furniture, though to what end was not clear. We thought better of asking, but we climbed the heather hill above the cottage for a late lunch in the lea of its amiable crouch. There are a couple of other croft houses, and Torran was back down on the shore of Loch Arnish, but there was no shred of activity on the ground. We had passed the time of day with a couple of young crofters half a mile back down the road, working their sheep, but here was the stillness of the grave. It is a calm place, Arnish, but sad. Sad for what has been lost which need not have been lost. A road hasn't always been a reliable lifeline for crofting communities, but the absence of one has usually been a reliable means of strangling a community. In my mind is a glen on Skye where the crofters eventually gave up the unequal struggle for the want of a road (and the want of a Calum Macleod in their midst), but years later, when a new landowner wanted to plant forestry, the road was in quick enough, and the builders used machines the size of houses, and they could have done with a lesson in the building of it all from Calum. For his is a credit to his island and theirs is a dire insult to Skye. Now Arnish has its road but it has not saved the north end. No one lives beyond here now, none on Raasay, none on the small tidal island of Fladday. South Rona has a new live-in owner and resettlement of a kind is in their long-term plan, but the road to Arnish is not likely to figure much in their scheme of things.

Mostly, the drift among the islands is still away, but there is the hint of a suggestion that an old tide is turning. The Scottish Crofters Union is a young organisation, the success of the Assynt crofters in buying their own land at a fair price has startled others all across the crofting counties into an awareness of what is possible. Raasay is in public ownership – under Highlands and Islands Enterprise – and if its two separate crofting philo-sophies of north and south can ever be fused to a single thread of purpose as single-minded as Calum's Road, anything is possible.

Raasay has been none too gently handled by its landlords in recent years, and although the vile spectre of Dr Green has now been exorcised, the spirit of Calum Macleod has yet to be invoked to the island's common purpose. It may be all that it would take to put the fate of Raasay where it has not been for a long, long time: back in the hands of its people.

Applecross was lost in a rage of storms. Skye was still switching itself off and on, dancing to the tune of the squall-wielding wind and the spotlight-ing sun. We walked back to the car discussing one aspect or other of the road, of crofting, of island life, pausing to admire the side-slip of a buzzard and the careless progress of a solitary red deer stag. Andy's eye would alight on a tiny plant clenched against winter and identify it as an incomer from New Zealand which had found a niche for itself and was prospering on the verge of Calum's Road.

I weighed the time against the niggardly span of daylight which the Hebridean midwinter affords, and proposed a brief drive down the island and a walk round to Hallaig. There was time, and neither of us minded the prospect of another cold soaking. It was a good decision. For the next two hours, winter paused. It was as if the mechanism propelling that violent chain reaction of storms down the northern ocean had stalled suddenly. The ensuing vacuum was filled by sunlight.

'The first thing you notice about Calum's Road is the way it fits the landscape, obeying contours. When you build by hand, you can do this'

*'The sea was the shade of glaciers . . . Hallaig was still and dreaming
and the only sounds were of distant waterfall and falsetto
raven . . .'*

The track was green, a ledge between cliff and sea with all Raasay's eastern seaboard at our disposal, a seaboard cleansed by all the day's storms and miraculously becalmed. The calm had not got as far as Applecross, but Kintail's far ridges were glittering and sharp. Then we paused and I turned and the Cuillin of Skye had emerged, vast and white and purpled by cloud shadows, and in that guise seemed to have advanced a mile northwards so that they trembled hugely over Raasay. At their feet, Scalpay flattened like an obedient dog and sunned itself.

I am never easy with the idea of turning my back on the Cuillin. There is such presence in their midst. They magnetise the senses in a way I have not encountered elsewhere. To turn and walk the other way has always felt like committing a fundamental breach of nature's laws. But this was Raasay's day and you can no more serve Bla Bheinn and Hallaig than you can God and Mammon. We turned our backs on Bla Bheinn and walked north purposefully for Hallaig.

Something flashed out on the Inner Sound, a host of pinpricks catching the sun, a dense shoal of sparks. It took a moment to make sense of such a compact mass of fragments, but the glasses revealed a frenzy of gulls on the surface of the water, presumably marking the presence of a shoal of small fish. A great slaughter was taking place. Andy, who is better at such things than I am, estimated 600 to 700 birds, but the mass of them was so dense that at its centre they obliterated the colour of the water entirely. To the naked eye, it looked like an exploding ice floe. In the glasses there was just enough detail to get a sense of the chaos of the flock, the frantic wings colliding, each bird pulsating as the wings of the bird above shadowed it for fleeting half-seconds, the sun striking between the shadows, that stuttering movement repeated on every other bird thousands of shadowing downbeats every minute. In a telescope, it would have been sensational. Without one, it was sensational enough to pull our eyes down from the mountain profiles, down through the wide sea miles and the scatter of islands to its single silvery focal point. We were too distant to hear a syllable of its fearful screech.

Hallaig's cliffs unfurl slowly before your eyes as you walk north, saving the grandest gestures for the last hidden curve in the track. Any four-season wanderer of Scottish islands pays nature's price for his pleasures. At any season, and especially in midwinter, he must lock horns with the weather and other discomforts and inconveniences, but he goes always like a pearl hunter for that moment when the protective shell cracks open and he grasps the unsullied jewel.

Such a moment appeared under Hallaig. The great shaggy wooded cliffs climbed from a silken, pale sea up through their tiers of rock and ancient forest to the summit of Dun Caan. Waterfalls gathered the sweetness of their pure springs and heaved it whitely out into the island air, down into the salt oblivion of the sound. The sea was the shade of glaciers, the woods dark and shadowed, but round the rim of Dun Caan's upstart crown and all along Raasay's high eastern edge the lowest of suns ignited the island's snowcap. From below, under Hallaig, it looked as if a miles-long strip of tinfoil had been fixed to the clifftop. The sunlight was to the south-west, but in the north, new forces of snowstorm were gathering, in skies the colour of fresh bruises.

For the moment, though, Raasay held them at bay. Hallaig was still and dreaming and the only sounds were of distant waterfall and falsetto raven.

The Raasay folk love to walk here, and for those who are so inclined, to quietly applaud the life of Sorley MacLean for the distinction he conferred on his native island. There is a low stone by the trackside where they were accustomed to sit and take all this in, quietly and with some gratitude. Here was as good a place as any to reinforce the belief that Raasay is the most beautiful place on earth.

But a small disservice has been done here. Whereas Calum's cairn at the top of his road is appropriate and well wrought, someone – not an islander, and uninvited – has seen fit to concrete a crude cairn on to the flat Hallaig-watcher's stone. Worse, Sorley's poem has been attached to the cairn on a flimsy tin plate which is slowly rusting and determinedly detaching itself. What is required here is a fit of conscience-troubling on the part of the cairn-builder, or a small bout of public-spirited vandalism to remove the wretched little thing from the landscape. It may be that in time the islanders would like a memorial to Sorley and his great poem, and it may be that they would not. If I were an islander I would hold that there is no finer monument than Hallaig itself, and no finer way of honouring poet and poem than by slipping a copy of it into my pocket and reading from a seat on the flat stone under the great cliffs:

> and when the sun goes down behind Dun Caan
> a vehement bullet will come from the gun of Love;
>
> and will strike the deer that goes dizzily,
> sniffing at the grass-grown ruined homes;
> his eye will freeze in the wood,
> his blood will not be traced while I live.

'And when the sun goes down behind Dun Cana a vehement bullet will come from the gun of Love' – Sorley MacLean

Chapter Eight

TALISKER, BRITTLE AND SNIZORT

WHENEVER LIFE PERMITS, I shake the mainland dust from my feet and head for Skye. Skye and I are such good friends now that we know and tolerate all each other's moods. There is no month and no extreme of good and ill fortune we have not shared. We travel great distances to meet each other.

I have climbed high to a land-locked mountain corrie where a dark lochan lies in the lap of ungarnished rock and I have smelled the sea and dreamed of Cuillin. On a shore of Angus or East Lothian or Sutherland I have seen a blue wave fall on pale sand buttressed by sea-wearied rock and I have invoked Talisker. On the upper reaches of the Forth west of Stirling I have watched Ben Ledi's evening pyramid darken past sunset, and in the lazing river and the distant mountain shape I have leapt in my mind to Skeabost where a track heads off into the moor and Ben Grasco skips up its craggy tiers.

Islands are rarely river places. In Skye I can think of a thousand burns but only a handful of rivers. Yet of that handful, three of them – the Talisker, the Brittle and the Snizort – spring as fondly to mind as any Skyescape. But none of them is merely river.

Talisker is four things: a bay, a place with three houses, a river, and the most sensational thing man ever distilled. Derek Cooper wrote memorably of an encounter with a distillery sample of 100-proof Talisker:

> The pungent, slightly oily, peaty ruggedness of the bouquet mounts in
> my nostrils. The corpus of the drink advances like the lava of the Cuillin
> down my throat. Then voom! Steam rises from the temples, a seismic
> shock rocks the building, my eyes are seen to water, cheeks aflame I

steady myself against a chair. Talisker is not a drink, it is an interior explosion, distilled central heating; it depth-charges the parts, bangs doors and slams windows.

The Talisker you buy in the pub or the off-licence is unlikely to be 100 proof. The earth is unlikely to move, although your mind might slip its moorings and cast off into the night. You might sip a large one in a basement howff in the gray heart of old Edinburgh and find you have Skye in the palm of your hand. I was keeping my own company in just such a howff, Talisker in hand, and in the way it sometimes goes with malt whiskies locked into landscapes of particular distinction, the dreary December outside was expunged from the world. My seat was not a bar stool beside a gas fire with artificial flames but a sun-warmed rock at the edge of Talisker Bay and in my mind was a day in April.

The River Talisker's life is short, sweet and eventful. It rises on a flank of Stockval, one of those flat-topped and crag-girt upthrusts which characterise so much of Skye's moorland interior. It flows gleefully west, headlong for the sea, spilling 150 feet in a mile of Gleann Oraid, tumbling between a dark cliff and Cnoc na h-Iolaire, which is Hill of the Eagle, keeping the road company.

But in its last mile it grows becalmed, for Talisker Bay is backed by something like a grassy delta. There are cliffs on all sides, it is true, but the bay is half a mile wide and facing west and the impression is of brightness and space rather than the containment of the cliffs. The river, though, hugs a corner of the bay, as though it is unwilling to leave the protective shadow of the cliff. Cliffs, after all, have shadowed its every movement from source to sea.

The burn which flows from Talisker House to the sea is dye-straight, primrose-painted and stravaigled by otters. A dipper's arrowhead zips seawards a foot above that golden-brown mile, close enough for the white breast of him to show as a pale blur in the water. Talisker is a fine house graced by that rarest of Skye flora, tall trees. Their flourishing crowns and spires make an eloquent point. It is to remind the island's self that it was once known for its woodedness. Better still, it preaches the landscape wisdom of trees in a largely treeless place. Portree, Dunvegan Castle and the eastmost strip of Sleat make the same point, but wilder Talisker under its cliffs makes it better.

The burn joins the river just above the shore. In its long canal-like course, the wide, grassy flatlands it bisects, the river and the shore, it is hard to imagine a more perfect place for otters. The seagoing otter of the islands is a much less coy creature than the furtive swimmer of the English river. Midday or midnight, dusk or dawn, burn or bank, sea or shore: the Skye otter is the ultimate all-rounder.

The musky language of spraints punctuates the bank of the burn. They say an otter has passed. If you have an eye practised at reading them, they can tell you how long gone the otter may be . . . long gone and the spraint is gray or white, brittle and scentless; just gone and it is wet and soft and musky. Flat rocks or grassy projections are favourite places. Five-toed footprints in the mud tell the same story. To an otter nose, they also tell which otter passed, and whether or not it had any business being there.

You see the otter at its amphibious best on a burn like this, narrow and low-banked. I saw him on my third consecutive morning walking the burn to the river to the sea. He was fifty yards ahead of me and weaseling along the bank. He rippled as he ran, and what with the sunlight and the trees he dappled as he rippled. His fur was pale and dry and thick, which is the otter most otter-watchers don't glimpse. He had been sunning himself, and was newly roused, ready for the hunt.

Brightness flooded the burn where the trees ended. He took to the water at once. It was, I thought, the last I would see of him, for my mind's eye had placed him swimming flat out for the river. Then I saw him, or at least the bubbly v-shaped wake of him, heading upstream, towards me. I pressed back against the nearest tree and waited. Be a tree, I told myself.

The otter was directly beneath me, six feet away as he swam past, the shadow of him swimming just ahead and to the left of him, up the bed of the burn. He curved towards a tiny slope on the further bank, cruised ashore and hit it running. He was twenty feet away and had his back to me when he stopped dead and turned his head and neck. One foot was half-raised, like a pointer, but he was pointing upstream and staring back at me. He was sleek and dark and streamlined, now barely recognisable as the animal of thirty seconds before. He uttered a single syllable, something between a grunt and a gasp, and with a movement as fluid as oil on marble, he uncurved and flowed into the burn and swam past me again. This time the shadow trailed a foot or two behind him.

For as long as he was underwater I could follow as quickly and noisily as I liked, ready to crouch and freeze as soon as I saw him surface. He surfaced, eighty yards ahead. I crouched and froze. He looked back from the water. He stepped out and looked back. He would see my crouch. But he was weasel too, and weasel means curiosity. He stood.

I love that. I caught myself smiling. Anything musteline, from a weasel to a badger, and including otters, vents its curiosity by standing tall and two-footed, the better to see and scent. It has the side-effect of making the animal look like what it is not. I see an otter 'stand' and I think of a toddler

wearing a nappy; a weasel on the move is a serious proposition, warrior and athlete in equal parts. But when he stops and stands he is a *Wind in the Willows* caricature of himself. My otter of Talisker stood.

In the glasses he showed himself to be an old beast, gray-muzzled and wearing lightly the wisdom of his years. He moved from water on to land and back without a break in his stride, without interruption to the fluidity and fluency of movement: he ran like a swimmer, swam like a runner. But he stood like a weasel.

I watched him watch me, then in the manner in which I have trained myself over the years, I reached out of myself with my eyes so that I could see our small confrontation and set it in the context of the Skye landscape. If I was eagle, what would I see?

I would see first the land fall away on all sides to the sea. I would see how that flat, green plain (plain at least by Skye's un-flat reckoning) softened and tamed river and burns born into the madness of the cliffs; see how slow they run over the flatland to the sea. On the smallest of these waters, just beyond the trees, there would be an otter, standing. The eagle is familiar enough with the otter, the otter with the eagle. They ignore each other.

The eagle would not be fooled by my crouch, would not need the otter's second glance. Out here, though, he would go fearlessly enough. He is in his element, and might dare as low as he wished hunting across the open ground. He can fly as low to the ground as the head of a standing otter or a crouching man, then leap up the air with godly indifference, throwing his shadow on the bald, dark forehead of Preshal which rears forever above Talisker in a single great cliff.

It is a landscape for godly gestures. Did not Cuchullin himself cross from Ireland in three strides, the third of them alighting on Talisker Point, carelessly breaking off a Sphynx-like piece of rock which remains to this day, staring forever west?

I have seen this eagle-of-my-mind before, watched it glide high over Preshal then slip down its network of airy zig-zags to the grassy bottom of Talisker, where it hunted the grasses, low as a harrier, then bounded away up the air again. As it climbed, readjusting the landscape, I tried to put my own eye in its mind. Every time I come to Talisker, which is often, I remember the eagle and I try again. I get no nearer the sense of it all than I ever did, but it is a good way to lift my eyes deliberately from a small,

PREVIOUS PAGE: *'The burn which flows seawards from Talisker House to the sea is dye-straight, primrose painted and stravaigled by otters...'*

low focal point to the high-sided arena of Talisker and its dome of sky. I returned my gaze to the otter.

He still stood, watching. I watched back. He dropped forward, and with two leisurely strides was back in the water, swimming away downstream, running the bank, swimming, running, in and out of the water with unbroken fluency. I was still in the same crouch when the otter cut away from the bank, took the shore at a leisurely lope, and without pause nosed into the first of the waves. I saw him porpoise once or twice out through the waves, but then he was in about the feet of the Sphynx, and I lost him.

At noon, the day grew calm, the wind withered, and the sun put the year's first true warmth on the day. I found a niche high on the north side of the bay, an easy ledge on the ragged cliff face, and I sat. On such a day in such a landscape, sitting is what I do best. I would become as stony as Cuchullin's Sphynx, as still as the ledge where I sat. I watched the sea's restlessness dwindle.

The blue of a Hebridean sea in April sunshine is an indefinable shade, several indefinable shades. Something of the kingfisher is in it, and something of the peacock. It darkens by degrees towards the horizon. The troughs of its small waves show as dark bands. That sand you thought of as white is nothing of the kind. That breaking wave is white, and in contrast the sand it washes is tawny and gray. The blue deepens as the sea westers. Islands shimmer where meandering mirages wobble the horizon. I let out an un-Sphynx-like sigh. If only heaven could look this good.

A single gull walked the shore, feeding desultorily. When it flew it took two forward steps and laid open its wings and rose perhaps two feet, glided a few yards then landed. It walked and fed some more, then two-stepped and glided again, and in that idling activity, whiled away the best part of an hour. In flight, it was a transformed creature, for the sun lined the leading edges of its stiff and down-curved wings with brilliant white, and put a cap of the same shade on its head. The top of its wings and its back glowed pearly gray, and its body was shadowed gray-blue by its own wings. Its red feet were stowed under the tail, lowered again only at the flight's last gasp. On it walked, dabbing at the wet sand, at the crevices between stones. Bird and slow sea were all that moved.

I had been on my ledge an hour when the kestrel arrived. I did not see where it came from, nor where it went, but it announced itself with a shriek, rounded an overhang on the cliff, thrust yellow legs towards my ledge, shrieked again, and in a slaister of burnt-orange and slate-gray wings it swerved frantically out from the rock face and dived down. The sun made it look like a fireball. Then there was nothing, apart from the fire nipping at every nerve-end in my body. I dare say it is rare enough for a kestrel to

find a Sphynx on its nesting cliff. It was hardly the nesting time for kestrels, not at Skye's latitude, although the bird could have been reconnoitring old haunts. I sat on. The nerve-ends dowsed.

Two hours slipped into three. The wind stirred. I had dozed briefly. I cast my eyes around Talisker Bay again, taking in Preshal, the burns, the dark mass of the Sphynx across the bay, the pale sand, the receding tide. My eyes drifted back to the rock behind the Sphynx, a small replica with an extra topknot. Something had changed. The topknot looked taller. Something large was sitting on it, something very large. My first thought was eagle, but it was hardly an eagle perch, not with the tide sucking and gnawing at its feet. I said aloud:

'Not eagle, at least not *golden* eagle . . .'

In my pack were my binoculars and my much-travelled, well-worn copy of Seton Gordon's 1929 classic *The Charm of Skye* (mine is the 1931 7s 6d edition). I unearthed them both, put them both to work. The glasses were inconclusive. A big bird certainly, but in silhouette and unflinching, I couldn't be certain of anything at that distance.

Seton Gordon has a chapter called 'Tallisker of the Rocks' (the only two–l spelling of it I have ever encountered). I quickly found what I was looking for:

> Let us climb to Biod Ruadh, where the rock falls sheer to the Minch a thousand feet beneath, and while yet the sun shines warm and Tallisker is free of showers, feast upon the vision of sea, hill, and isle . . . On a grassy ledge of the precipice is the ancient eyrie of a sea-eagle. Its owners have gone; indeed there is not one pair of these birds nesting in Britain at the present day.

Ah, but that was then. A tide has turned for sea-eagles and they nest in the islands again thanks to the endeavours of the NCC and the RSPB and the careful nurturing of young birds on Rum. There is Rum across a few miles of sea, nothing more than a languorous glide for a sea-eagle. Besides, they have spread far beyond Rum, and there are Skye headlands and cliff faces where their curious terrier-yap and mighty silhouette are famously familiar again. It was from a Skye eyrie in 1916 that the last sea-eagle flew wild. It was in 1985 that it next happened from a secret island ledge.

I put down the book and took up the glasses again, all torpor gone, the

OPPOSITE: *Talisker Bay, April: 'if only heaven could look this good . . .'*

---

nerve-ends aflame again. I had seen the sea-eagle on Skye, but not here, not here where Seton Gordon had earmarked the old eyrie ledge. He would have seen the last sea-eagle of them all before persecution drove them off the face of the land, for he lived on Skye for much of his life. He would doubtless have raged against its demise too, but he was too much the gentleman to rage in print. 'The sea-eagle has shared the fate of the osprey and other of our rare birds . . . ' That was all he noted. But he was a great champion of eagles, and had he been on my ledge that spring of 1990, his pulse would have quickened.

Still I could not convert my suspicions into certainty.

'What I need here,' I told myself, 'is a pair of crows.'

There are times when nature is a perverse sod in the company of its champions. There are also times when it behaves like an angel, and you sit on your ledge and feel like Mother Nature's favoured son. She conjured not a pair of crows but four of them, flying fast down the cliff face making straight for the turned back of the stranger in their midst. At the first two passes the perched bird simply ducked its head. At the third and fourth and fifth it adopted a horizontal standing posture rather than a vertical sitting one, then during a brief lull in the onslaught it flew.

The word 'flew' barely describes the action. There was a single raised flap of a pair of wings the size and shape of a wardrobe door. There was a banking turn round the nose of the great Sphynx, there was a touch of sunlight on the unmistakable white tail and only the second sea-eagle I had ever seen was gone in five flying seconds. The crows alighted on the shoreline rocks and bellowed.

'Couldn't you have sent it this way?' I asked them. There are times when nature is a perverse sod.

I had been on my ledge four hours. The west was marshalling salvoes of steely showers. I descended and walked back up the River Talisker to the road well content with my day in heaven . . .

. . . I drained my glass. The gas fire danced in its fake grate. A woman I did not know was sitting at the other side of the fire and looking at me and laughing.

'I'm sorry,' she said. 'I didn't mean to laugh. But you've been smiling at that fire for about five minutes.'

I grinned and held up the empty glass.

'I was in Skye,' I said.

Outside it was still December and Edinburgh, a combination I like well enough. But inside I was April and Talisker and the flagstones of the close were a rocky causeway between a cliff and a Sphynx.

Glen Brittle is the Cuillin climber's glen, or the Cuillin watcher's. Summers, it is a madness of tents and I would go a long way to avoid it. But in February, with a gale hammering upstream from the sea lifting waterspouts up Loch Brittle and into the mouth of the River Brittle, you can walk alone there and share your day only with eagle and buzzard and raven and the most compulsive mountain landscape in the land.

I love to pause at that high right-angle two-thirds of the way up Glen Brittle's monumental hill. The ground falls beneath you to the river, down among the winter-weary dull brown moors, then heaves up a vast slope to the gabbro-and-snow might of Coire na Creiche, northmost gulp of that icy upheaval which shaped the Cuillin.

If you were to chance on the River Brittle for the first time from the sea where it eases flatly into its sea loch you would be astounded by its tempestuous beginnings. Is there anything more elementally primitive and raw than the high corries of the Cuillin? It is in the Corrie of Thunder and the Corrie of the Wolf, watched over by the Peak of the Pipes, and foregathering in the Corrie of Pillaging, that the headwaters of the Brittle stir. The ridges and pinnacles of the Cuillin may be the exclusive preserve of seasoned and steady-headed climbers, but many of the corries are exhilarating walks into landscapes which non-rockhounds tend to think of as forbidden territory. Go carefully and respectfully and learn the magic of gabbro under your hands and feet. Walk among the great set pieces of the Ice as architect. Island Scotland has nothing else like it.

Coire na Creiche is hardly a tranquil corner of Skye, what with thunder and skirl and wolf-howl cacophonous in the mind, a south-westerly gushing frantically up the glen, throwing waterfalls head over their own heels, and the clamour of countless mountain burns. The mountains, with a week of snow thickly plastered into gullies and headwalls and edging ridges, and lambasted by the plasterer gales, rage up into a stupendous frontier. Behind them, unseen, but sensed by all who know the Cuillin well, the main ridge curls away south to Loch Scavaig like a loosely coiled landscape snake. For all the overawing tumult of the Cuillin from the banks of the Brittle below Coire na Creiche, it is only the tip of the tail of the snake.

The water is as greenish as glaciers on such a winter's morning, as cool on the throat as ice, as sweet on the tongue as honeycombs. There are no dull sensations here.

To walk upstream is a heady trek. Waterfalls stumble over each other, and each time you lift your eyes from that mesmerism the great Cuillin snake-tail has advanced and you crane hypnotically up into its repertoire of rock and snow astonishments. Then at your feet a new waterfall hurtles its cataract so far out from the course of the mainstream that a sleeker, less

*Swans, like Skye, are an addiction in my life . . . a whooper swan
'poses' during filming against the ridge of Sgurr Thuilm*

The film-star swans in their Citroën caused quite a stir on Skye in February

athletically ambitious branchline waterfalls beneath it, a fall within a fall. To compound that small miracle, a dipper nips out from behind the second fall where he has been prospecting for food, his ears dinned between the throats of the falls and the cold heartbeat of the rock.

It is at moments like this, peering into one more gouged-out slit-trench of riverbed down fifty feet of water-smoothed rock, that you see the moor for the first time in its true guise. It is not an interminable depth of peat, not here. It is a skin on the mountain rock. Like all skins it is winter-pallid and at its most susceptible to onslaught. The wind howls, high snow loosens, the burns gorge, the gabbro smooths some more, a poorly rooted patch of moor fails to cling on and crumbles into the irresistible maw of one more spate. On and on it goes, every moment of every year. Every moment there is a little less Cuillin than there was. Every moment there is a little more Cuillin stature in my eyes.

There have been many winter days in Glen Brittle, but only one that I shared with a pair of swans. Swans, like Skye, are an addiction in my life, an addiction which fuelled my 1992 book, *Waters of the Wild Swan*. That book, in turn, became the raw material for a television programme produced by the BBC's Natural History Unit in Bristol, hence the swans in Glen

Brittle. While I was filmed in Edinburgh and Glen Dochart, two of the book's settings, the swans were making their way to Skye, slowly and undecorously in the back of a Citroen Dyane. Whooper swans are common enough on the lochans of Skye through the winter. Mostly, though, they do not cruise across the island on wheels. Word quickly got around, especially after Andy Currie's wee piece in the *West Highland Free Press*. The swans were instant celebrities, their small entourage a cause of some comment and curiosity.

It was in Glen Brittle that we found the stretch of road and the kind of backdrop which would produce the kind of effect the producer required. The roof of the car was rolled back, their handler stood in the back with the cameraman. The tailgate was flipped open, the swans jumped down, the car drove off, the handler flapped his arms and made encouraging noises, the swans ran and took off and flew, and they followed the car. As they followed, they were filmed, and as they were filmed, the snow-strewn Cuillin slid seductively through the viewfinder.

It was not quite as easy as I have made it sound. The road is a switchback and the wind was a gale that made standing difficult even on solid gabbro. The swans sometimes whipped away on the wind, or hammered up the updraughts, or were knocked sideways and recovered their equilibrium half a mile from the car. It was cold, and as with all filming there were waits and frustrations and failures. But for a week and a bit I was in the company of a small group of people and a pair of swans and an eccentric car, and the memory of it now is that it was never less than warm and funny and enthralling.

The memory I hold dearest, though, is the sight of whooper swans in flight, far out over the glen, turning to answer a human voice, turning to home in on our small, beckoning knot, hurtling down the wind to pass low overhead, bugling brassily as they flew over, turning into the wind to circle again and land on the riverbank. The circling of one bird crossed the great white wedge of Sgurr Thuilm, and there, with its wings high and tail feathers lit by the most fleeting and flimsiest of suns, I photographed it.

I have never thought of out-of-season Glen Brittle as anything less than complete, what with its mountain shapes and its river and its sea door and its eagles. But I have now seen it with the extra dimension of swans, albeit implanted ones, and I love the place the more because of them. It is an irrational response because Glen Brittle is hardly a swan thoroughfare, and I will almost certainly never see swans there again.

Nature could not resist a pointed reminder of the natural scheme of things. I had driven cameraman Andrew Anderson back up the glen after one filming run, and as I drove I enthused about the flight powers of the birds in the face of such a wrecking wind. Just as we pulled into the lay-by we had commandeered at the top of the hill, I noticed an eagle low over the plantation. Andrew got out to watch while I reached for my camera. I was out ten seconds behind him, having paused to change lenses frantically. Andrew's measured voice said:

'I shouldn't bother, Jim, he's 2,000 feet higher than the last time you saw him.'

So he was. We had interrupted his hunting, and he had responded by soaring almost vertically for (I agreed with Andrew's instant estimate) about 2,000 feet. We watched as he dipped a few hundred feet, half folded his wings and bulleted off across the mountainside in a shallow, upwind dive. Now *that* was flying in the face of such a wind, the native in his native element, the master of all its winds rather than a combatant striving in unequal struggle.

Still, I consoled my swan-ardour, I wonder if anyone has ever watched an eagle and a swan before, over the same Skye river in the same hour. Then I remembered: yes, I had . . .

Skye wept. My third consecutive September day dawned like the first two, as reluctant as a hedgehog in January, as sluggish as a duck in mud. Rain flowed in vertical tides, warm and windless, soft and ruthless from first light to last. The high moor above Bracadale oozed like a sponge through every peat-black pore. The Snizort, never the most expressive of rivers, swole and girned at its trembling banks with barely suppressed ill-tempered power. It wouldn't take much . . .

I made what I could of such an island day by following the angler's path deep into the moor. I found the river's mood catching. It is a way of meeting such days head on, not to try to shout nature down in its sullen moods but immerse yourself in what you find. Let nature pull you down with it, and go compassionately hand in glove with its moroseness. So I broke my own silence only to curse the sodden land's underfoot treacheries where I fell foul of them. A straight line short-cut across one of the river's long loops was a bad idea. An over-trousered leg sank up to its over-trousered thigh. By the time I had extricated myself I wore the colour and equilibrium of temperament of a rutting stag without hinds, and there was nothing the river's mood could teach me about moroseness.

On, if only for a way of passing the day. Tomorrow may be a gem, I told myself for the third time in three days, and I would have this day's weary drapery to set it against, the more to admire its finery. September is the best of it in the islands, when it is true to itself, the slack water in the ebb and flow of the seasons. It lies like a brimful tidal pool amid the rock

'*I marvelled at quicksilver Skye and the way it turns its landscape
tears to sequins stitched to its matchless glittering flair . . .*'

*Skye's rivers rise and flow and fall to the sea, the silken threads of
a web which ensnares the very fabric of the island*

and wrack of the wild year, betraying barely either a trace of the ebb of summer or the gathering forces of the flow of autumn. But that true-to-itself September is a rarity in the islands, and it is as likely to throw you four seasons in any one day as the yellow and poised and flat calm September you crave.

Five mallards leapt from my path, doubtless as much from astonishment as from alarm. I followed their flight for as long as my eyes could hold on to it in the murk, the only other moving fragments of the morning, apart from me and the rain and the river's inexorability. They circled back over-head, the drakes quacking like every cartoon duck you ever heard. I fumbled for the glasses, caught up with the birds fifty yards downstream, lost them to the circling, drenching curtains of mist and rain, and decided that freeing the glasses from the pack was not worth the effort.

But they were out now, and I swung them through the points of the compass in a slow sweep of the horizon-less world. Somewhere between north and south-south-east (who knows in *this*?), they dragged my eyes past a discernibly mobile fragment of low hillside. I had found a moor-quartering golden eagle by the most absurd of flukes.

My friend Mike Tomkies once offered me a piece of priceless advice about watching for golden eagles in eagle country: 'Learn to scan the middle distance.' It was never so easy as that day on the Snizort – there was only middle distance. I have often had cause to value Mike's friendship. Now, as I focused on that spread-eagling of dark wings rendered huge by the perspec-tive-less light, the day's burdens avalanched from my shoulders.

I watched her (I decided she was female on the basis of her great size, a hasty judgment given I had only mallards to compare her with) work the ground for ten minutes, crossing and re-crossing the same hill slope as diligently as a ploughman. She was never higher than six feet above the moor, often less. She did not touch it once. The wings barely moved. The control of flight was astonishing, as astonishing in its minute adjustment and buoyancy as that single 2,000-foot leap in Glen Brittle. Restraint, flawless fluency, calculated purpose – she was everything the river was not.

I followed her in the glasses until my eyes and arms ached, and still I followed her. The rain was inside every layer of clothing by now, and what wasn't wet with rain was wet with perspiration. I consoled myself that the eagle was wetter, and still she stayed close, and still she hunted, and still I held her in the gray circle of the glasses, Once she tipped a wing and fell to within inches from the ground, so low and slow now that she must land. But she checked even that small descent, laid open her wings and let whatever it is that lifts an eagle a foot above the ground lift her. It was a last gesture. She had exhausted the slope's possibilities and cut up through the cloying curtains and the rain, and she was gone. I was left alone with the river and my thoughts.

It is not hard to see eagles in Skye once you know where to look and what it is you are looking for. The island has a healthy eagle population, all the rock ledges of an eagle paradise, and many a moorland mile for good eagle hunting. Even so, the chances of a solitary, wandering man and a solitary, wandering eagle occupying the same quarter-of-a-square-mile for ten unbroken minutes are not high in that weather or any other.

The change began in the north. First the rain eased, then it stopped. The mist curtain receded, then began to dematerialise. I felt wind on my face, light and cool, and responded at once by peeling off my outer waterproof layer. It was like stepping from a chrysalis and discovering flight. The sky over Rona was yellow. I turned and saw blue in the north-west, then in the south. To the east, diminishing by the moment, was a retreating wall of deep black. I took a compass bearing from the edge of a small plantation and headed through the last of the mist for the high ground of the moor, a small, flat-topped crag 1,200 feet up and perfectly poised to watch the afternoon emerge. As I reached the crag, the sun tunnelled through and I sat and ate and drank and marvelled at quicksilver Skye and the way it turns its landscape tears to sequins stitched to its matchless glittering flair.

In an hour, Skye was again an island on the edge of the Minch. It was the shape I knew and loved. The Western Isles lay hard and meticulously etched on a sea-and-sky horizon of unfathomable clarity. Dark and tiny silhouettes impossible distances west pricked other horizons. St Kilda, perhaps ninety miles away. Two hours ago, it was down to about ninety yards.

I returned to the river. There, by a reedy fold, it had grown blue and demure and submissive. In the morning it had been turgid and overbearing. Where there had been a prison of rains there was the distant blue skyline of the Cuillin. They rose from the born-again moor like pyramids from desert sand, and the Snizort seemed to uncoil all the way back to their implausible foothold on the island. It does no such thing, of course, for it is a moorland river, born and bred, and knows no mountain wellspring, but deceptions were swimming across the island now as thick as rainclouds on the morning. Every new yard turned my head. Skye danced, and I danced with it.

If my day's walking had been a haphazard affair thus far, these last few steps down off the moor were surely the stuff of predetermination. There in midstream were the heads (all that was visible above tall banks) of two whooper swans, bills vivid yellow and tipped black, crowns stained rusty yellow from feeding in the peat waters of their Icelandic homeland. They

called and wheeled, and at once four more swans were beside them. The calling grew anxious, they swam fast past me to a straighter stretch of water and with six short strides they were airborne. They flew, white spirits of my wilderness, following the watercourse upstream, deep into the heart of the moor.

You do not think of Skye as a river place. But when you think of how its rivers rise and how they flow and fall to the sea, they become the silken threads of a web which ensnares the fabric of the island. At their best they are Talisker, Brittle and Snizort, and none of them is merely river.

PREVIOUS PAGE: *'Rain flowed in vertical tides, warm and windless, soft and ruthless . . .'*

Chapter Nine

THE HEADLAND OF THE STRANGER

YOU CAN DO this on Mull: drive off the ferry at Craignure, straight up the east coast of the island to Tobermory, along Tobermory's technicolour main street, and when you can drive no further, get out and walk, walk straight off the end of the street into a tunnel of trees and keep walking until you emerge from the trees and see the lighthouse. With no effort on your part, you have changed planets.

It is a good place to begin, or to begin again. Rubha nan Gall is the Headland of the Stranger. Mull and I are familiar strangers. We take up where we left off after lapses of years. The addiction craves not just islands but the diversity of islands and the journeying. Mull is within easy reach. I have tended towards trickier shores, or Skye of course, always Skye. So I save Mull for another day, but sooner or later I remember trees in an island setting, the splendidly isolated Ben More, the high eagle-haunted terraces above Calgary Bay, the secretive valley of Lochbuie (and because Mull is much more than one island), the Iona Blue, the scattered buckshot of Treshnish, the low-slung dark hull of Staffa, sunset-smitten Ulva . . . I remember all that and I want to walk off the end of the main street again and stand on the Headland of the Stranger.

I think of February. That February I had reached Mull on the first of a two-day lull in a season of storms. The day before's north-easterly had off-loaded vast cargoes of snow. Ben More was hull-down in it, but suddenly the wind had inhaled and held its breath. The sky was that postcard blue you decline to believe in when you see it in a souvenir-shop window. The clouds were the stuff of children's drawings, small and sparse and scattered and fluffed up and no more credible than the sky. Mull's stockpile of white hills lay beneath it all, fuelling impatience in the ferry queue at Oban. The

'The lighthouse stands at the end of Mull's most astonishing mile . . .'

The mountains of Mull may not be as towering as the song suggests
but they have their quiet winter moments

crew toiled oblivious to it all, doing nothing constructive to the stranger-eye, nothing to assist our departure a moment before schedule at noon, so I walked to the pier railing and photographed Mull-in-waiting and prayed for an afternoon as godsent as the morning. And I wondered why I had let myself become a stranger again.

The lighthouse stands at the end of Mull's most astonishing mile. At the beginning is Mull's most famous street (its only street, in truth). Here is as much bustle as Mull can muster, which in February amounts to something on the relaxed side of hectic. But I had a trying, snowy, 200-mile drive, a broken exhaust, a ferry crossing and a CalMac chicken-salad sandwich to contend with. The end of that singular street had loomed large on the day's horizon.

The tree-tunnel snaffles you from the street. Instead of sea salt the place smells of musty leaves and hedgehogs. Thrushes oust the harbour stridencies of gulls. That softly dark tunnel performs the role of a decompression chamber, preparation for wilder, more elemental worlds beyond, a filter which entraps the impurities of mainlander travel like fallen leaves impaled on thorns. The sea glimpsed between winter-thinned branches and fifty feet below begins to assume those Hebridean hues you remember of old, the last time you were a stranger. The tunnel bends and in the light at its end there is a lighthouse, a Hebridean sea, a mountain.

. . . I have stopped beyond the trees. The landscape makes you do that. The distance belongs to Ardnamurchan, more Hebridean than West Highland, more an island with a land-bridge than a peninsula. The farthest distance, that shape over Ardnamurchan's dipping ocean-going shoulder, is Rum. The sky has deepened its shade and grown taller and wider. The clouds batter across it like dodgems, tiny, self-propelled things. The sea is dark blue and restless, calm only in the lighthouse bay. The sun is vividly on Ardnamurchan, on the scraps of cloud, on the sea, hazily on far Rum. The steep shore of the Sound of Mull where I stand is in deepest shadow. All that is lit here, lit more vividly than anything else on this new and rarefied planet beyond the tunnel, blazing more whitely than any mountain snows, the irresistible focal point of the landscape, is the lighthouse. You would think a great landscape painter, a Turner perhaps, had been summoned here to stand at the edge of the trees and advise the island how and where it might site the lighthouse so that it might be perfectly lynchpinned to its landscape of ocean backwater and cradling mainland. Turner might have looked at it all on such a February afternoon as this, noted where the sun threw the shadow of the cliff, noted the last bare rock beyond the shadow, and pointed: 'There – right in the middle of the canvas.' And there it stands, to gladden the eye of the returning stranger and beckon him out of the woods down to the island-ness of the shore.

There were 103 years of lighthouse keepers here until automation in 1960. I went down to reacquaint myself with their small domain. The old keepers' cottages are in that curious Siamese-twin relationship, joined by their back walls rather than their gables, an arrangement frequently used among the lights of the west. They are privately owned now, and drabber than they would ever have been allowed to become in their lightkeeping days. The light itself glitters unblemished white, an ignored shining example. A sign warns of 'disease precautions', advises against further exploration by strangers. Fair enough. I don't believe a word of it, but in any case the lighthouse is more compelling by far.

The shallows among the dark rocks held the light's wavering reflection. My lynchpinning notion was well served by that white glimmer, for there was the tower of the lighthouse burrowing down among the very rocks of Mull. It looked for that February moment as deep rooted as the splayed pyramid of Ben Haint across the sound on Ardnamurchan.

An oystercatcher touched down by the lighthouse reflection, not a dozen yards from where I sat. He was the dark of the rock, the white of the lighthouse, the scarlet of blood. I told him aloud:

'You owe your scarlet neb and legs to your forebears who waded in the sea at Bloody Bay a mile up the shore there, ae day in 1480, when the cannons of great ships roared and after the battle the tide came ashore red. From that day to this, all oystercatchers have red legs and red nebs.'

But he had put his blood-bill into the feathers of his back, and lifted one blood-leg and closed his eyes. You feel less of a stranger on the headland of Rubha nan Gall when an oystercatcher goes to sleep in your shadow.

I drained all the sunlight from that afternoon. The light stayed late on Ardnamurchan and on snowy Beinn Dubh while my own shore darkened and chilled. The tunnel of trees has a quite different effect on the stranger when you retrace your steps from the lighthouse. Your impatience has gone. You have been made welcome by the headland named after you. Tobermory is no longer the distant object of your impatience but a benign bay a mile from the lighthouse which shines even when it is not lit. Whatever it is which lights your path, there is no darkness in the wood now.

Trees are part of what it is which sets Mull apart. The chorus of the island's best-known traditional song throws in a bit of predictable tourist-board-ish bombast before the lines

Green grassy island of sparkling fountains
Of waving woods and high towering mountains

*Calgary in February is exquisite: sunlight 'seeps through like water
through a sponge, in points of light, thousands of them . . .'*

*Calgary's old and derelict pier: 'it wades into the sea in exquisitely
worked pink granite . . .'*

Poetic licence has been at work here (and leaning heavily towards the licence and away from the poetic): it's no more grassy than most islands, I have yet to see a fountain anywhere, the mountains don't really do much towering, but in places the woods do wave. In a Hebridean context, where weather and abuse of land have razed most woods to seaweed level, the survival of woods tall enough to wave is of no meagre significance. It is just as true that most of the waving woods need rather more urgent care and management and rather less grazing by sheep and deer than they experience at the moment, or a hundred years from now there will be scarcely a wood to wave on the island which has not been planted by the Forestry Commission. All too many a Mull hillside has felt the sourest jab of Commission monoculture on its fair face. Surely on this of all islands, the Commission might be expected to do better by way of honouring Mull's native woodland tradition. It's not that the Commission doesn't have its visionaries, just that all too often the system stultifies and blinkers their vision. Turn someone loose on Mull who knows the worth of its landscape and will treat it and its trees accordingly. Start with the high hill walls around Calgary and the magical secret valley which butts on to Lochbuie, and start before it's too late to do anything with Mull's waving woods but turn them into kitchen furniture.

That wind which had held its breath over the Sound of Mull began to exhale again over Calgary 24 hours later, a slow stirring at first, but colder and ever more hearty as the afternoon dwined down to the dusk. The woods at the back of the bay waved. Likewise the tortured pines which still cling to their pathetic survival up the steep slopes above the bay's north shore. Sheep and wind have done their worst there and where fencing would help the trees, the only fences in sight are for the safety of sheep. The same old lesson, unlearned all across Scotland, is unlearned in Mull.

Still, Calgary in February is exquisite. The trees climb to the snowline, the snow covering is just light enough to pick out the most precise detail, like a perfect etching, and the wind has worked up enough muscle to lift it in flimsy spindrifts from the small ridges. The sea falls back and the pale sands widen. The sun, which has flirted with the day, has lowered into a horizon-clinging cloud bank. But with the sun behind it, frailties emerge. It is not so much a bank as gray floss. The sun seeps through it like water through a sponge, in points of light, thousands of them. But it puts nothing like sunlight on the land and the sea is an unshining and unfathomable shade you would call neither dark nor pale with any confidence. The intensity of the hillside snow is all that deepens and glows under such a fractured sun. Under such a February afternoon Calgary Bay has grown private and alone.

Summer tourism claims and acclaims this place. A few years ago the hordes had to be ushered off the machair where cars and tents were layering the beauty of the place with the ugliest tides of erosion. It is a frail plain, the machair, but at Calgary it has begun to heal now. There is a good lesson there for the waving woods.

No tourist walks the pier track round the edge of the bay in February. A Land-Rover pick-up is at the end of the track, the shepherd's boots and the collie's paws imprint the mud. The sign which screams NO DOGS from a gate implicitly exempts the collie.

I followed that workaday spoor trying to catch the new mood of the late afternoon, ordering stray scraps of landscape in my mind, shepherding instincts. In the last hour, Mull had grown subdued and subtle, dispelling the blue mood of the Headland of the Stranger. I reached out for the sense of the changed island as I walked.

Calgary Bay is a contained place. In the failing light its sidewalls grow immense, darkening and seeming to stand forward a pace. They deal in substantial gestures, broad terraces, scooping climbs, high headlands. From the beach at the head of the bay the Atlantic is implausible, distant, something which passes by the far mouth of the bay, under that cloud sponge. But the further you walk, the higher up the terraces you climb, you see the horizon widen, the scalps of other islands align themselves across the west. The waters of bay and ocean commingle and overlap, quietude and agitation nudging each other across the rocks of Rubha nan Oirean, the Headland of the Border. That long, gray shapelessness under the cloud is Coll; that stutter of fantastical shapes fading into softer focus as they wester . . . that is Treshnish. It is, after all, the ocean which reclaims that tide falling down the fair sands of Calgary. It is nearer than you might think.

A small, dark, erect shape catches your eye from the sands; a figure, a standing stone? It stands far out along the central terrace which bisects the north shore's long cliff. It is a stone rather than a figure, and it is standing. Whether or not it's a standing stone though, rather than a volcanic fragment spat out and embedded on end, would take a more educated guess than mine. If it is a standing stone, its erectors toiled to good effect to make it conspicuous from a great distance. It stands by the rim of a small and shallow bowl, a green crater, with, at its heart, a low mound. Does the stone commemorate the mound? I hope so, but maps and text-books are silent. I walked on out to a small shelf of the headland with a fulmar's-eye view of the ocean. You see past Treshnish Point from here, a sightline which unwraps the full quirky regiment of line-abreast rock shapes. If you want them line astern, you must cross the bay and claw over a moorland mile to the hummock of Cruachan Treshnish, from which vantage point they make even less sense.

I let my eye wander the darkening ocean while my mind scavenged fruitlessly among the landscapes' shapes for clues, clues to indicate how nature at its most violent might have contrived a sunken, smooth oval round a perfect mound in the midst of a cliff terrace then pitched a headstone headlong on to its end, so that it embeds on the rim of its handiwork. Such things are possible, of course. But I know that if I was an ancient chieftain of stone hewers with all Mull's western seaboard at my disposal for my last resting place, I would opt for this high brim of Calgary Bay, the hills and waving woods at my back, a pair of drifting eagles a thousand feet above my head and an ocean wind to bear my spirit to Tir Nan Og.

The darkest rock frown of that shore has a name – A' Charraig. It is a dangerous game, plucking definitions from Gaelic dictionaries when your knowledge of the language is on the monosyllabic side of conversational. But Dwelly's, the definitive, first-base Gaelic reference work, offers an intriguing possibility among several definitions, one of which fits the setting perfectly: 'Rock jutting into the sea serving as a quay or fishing station . . .'

Below the cliff is a pier, and between the cliff and the pier there plunges a basalt dyke, a weird outcrop quite unlike any other rock on that hillside. Where it peters out on the shore, some marvellously instinctive and unsung stoneworker has built on to its embedded strength. There is only a shell of the old pierhouse now, which is sad, although there is shell enough to show his ingenuity. But what has happened to the pier is shameful. Its landward end is the same dark rock as the shore, but it wades into the sea in exquisitely worked pink granite. Such granite can only have been hewn from the coast around Fionnphort and Kintra on the Sound of Iona and ferried round the coast to Calgary by someone willing to labour extravagantly to wed the functional with art. Even the pierhead capstans are pink granite, small standing stones set into the pink paving, and as solid now as they were the day they were set. Handsomely cut steps reach down to the water, also fashioned from the same rosy shade.

Nature has rewarded such endeavour with her own definition of colour-coding, splashing and patching the pink with vivid canary-yellow lichen, the one primary colour in all Calgary that February afternoon. What is shameful is that the pier has been permitted to fall into treacherous decay, that the highest endeavour of earlier centuries of craftsmen has been rewarded not with the accolade of conservation but with a grotesque barbed-wire fence and a crude old Ministry of Agriculture and Fisheries sign, both of which say keep off in the most uncompromising terms. I say why? I crossed the fence and was beguiled by the stonework.

I raged at such dismissive neglect. We marvel, rightly, at such as Mousa broch or Jarlshof's multi-layered settlement and we protect and revere them.

Reudle schoolhouse: 'uncharacteristically tall, an affecting presence on its huge moorland plinth . . .'

But we snub this pier, presumably because it is not old enough to be revered. I say it is a marvel, and it is beautiful. I suggest this: a small group of Mull's unemployed might labour there under the tutelage of a stone-mason and learn to admire the humble craft of their forebears. In the process they will restore the pier and when one more body of tourism descends for one more Calgary summer there will be something new and also old and dignified to marvel at, out on Calgary Bay. And when that tourist season is past, the Mull people themselves can wander out quietly in their midwinter ones and twos and quietly admire the genius who toiled in their midst and wrought such dignity in stone on such a landscape.

So I walked out on to the pier and sat on a pink-granite capstan and took pleasure in the discovery that the neighbourhood otters also defy the fence and the notice and use the pier for their own purposes. I spent the last hour of the light on the top step, scribbling and photographing and thinking and watching an otter catching eels. I remember few more contented hours anywhere.

Where we *must* build amid nature's masterpiece landscapes, the highest compliment we can pay is to build beautifully, take pains to honour the landscape setting. The pier-builders took such pains, but their endeavours have been undone by the most thoughtless gestures of ugliness, and by permitting the decay of their work. It should be made beautiful again. Who cares if no one uses the pier? Who uses a broch?

The winter moor south of Calgary sprawls south up a couple of wide climbing miles, a quiet antidote to the spectacle of the bay. The eye moves restlessly across the moor for focal points, finds none. Then, near the high point of the road, there is the house. It stands roofless and alone a quarter of a mile from the road. For its age and its rooflessness and its isolation, you would expect such a house to be low to the ground, one more mute memorial to the Clearances. This one is two-storeyed, uncharacteristically tall, an affecting presence on its huge moorland plinth. The underfoot moor is a vile bog at first, but then there is the semblance of an old footpath. There had to be something with such a house. The path leads to the door, but the door is in the gable and the ground-floor windows are too many and too tall. This was not a house at all, but a school. Without looking for it, I had found Reudle.

The obvious question: if this was the school, where were the homes of the pupils? The track beckons you on up to the watershed of the moor, towards the sea. As I walked, the wind fell away again, the sun trembled then stilled and bore down on the moor, and February contrived something like spring for an hour either side of a golden noon.

All over the West Highland seaboard and among the islands there are moorland paths like this, crossing watersheds between the road and the shore, linking invariably empty townships with the road. Once they were lifelines. Now they are still-lifes. Over and over again, they say the same thing, mutter under their moorland breath posterity's protest at the grotesque darkness of the Highland Clearances. They have something else in common, these seaward paths. It is that you walk in the certainty of that climactic moment when the moor falls below your feet and the world is redefined by the colour and the shape and the light of the sea. It might happen after a mile or five miles, but the trick is revealed at the same critical point of the path, and in a handful of paces. I never tire of it, and I never fail to wonder at what the islanders made of it when they walked such paths for a living.

So the moor above Reudle schoolhouse relented and there was the sea, and the thumbprint of the Dutchman's Cap leading the skein of the Treshnish Islands south-west into the ocean like so many geese. In the warm tranquillity of that hour, it would have been easy to be an islander of that small sea valley. No eye could be indifferent to such a landscape for a threshold.

The village lay halfway between the watershed and the sea, the same low, dark walls, the same curved corners which quietened the wind, the same blend of the picturesque and the raw pain. There is no getting used to it. If there is Celtic blood in you, you bleed for the people of the Clearances all your days and there is nothing you can do about it.

Nearer the sea is a second village, quarter of a mile from the first and almost on the cliffs. This is Glacgugairidh, thoughtfully named, the Hollow of the Dark Grazings. An unlikely survivor, an ash tree, is infamous for the villager who hanged himself from its branches. The wonder is that there was only one.

Two hundred people lived here once. The children crossed the brackeny mile to the school and back with the winter sunrise on the Atlantic or the sting of squalls on their face. Now there is a hoodie-crow on the ash, there is a snipe prodding among the ruins (he is up at my approach, fast and low between two gables, hurdling a low wall, a rough screech in his wake as though a piper had hefted the bag and was about to tune up, but there has been no piper here in more than a hundred years) and there is everywhere the gray curse of sheep.

David Craig's brilliant and beautifully written investigation, *On the Crofters' Trail*, is harrowing on Mull:

> In 1848 and 1849 alone 600 families were warned out on Mull. The nationwide campaign by Highland landlords at that time was described by the chief government relief officer, who had the incredible name of Pine Coffin, as aiming at 'the extermination of the population'. Tobermory was a main transit camp for the refugees . . . and its population rose by eleven per cent, while Mull's fell by more than a quarter, during the Famine and its aftermath.

And David Craig was told this all too typical Clearances story:

> There was a Campbell who spoke up for the people against Forsyth when he was doubling and trebling the rents. He wanted them to sell their horses. Now, if there was a foal, they *needed* the two of them for ploughing. Campbell refused to sell, and some of the estate workers cut up his horses.

Tourism would often rather suppress such stories than own up to them. Political sensitivities intervene here and there, even now, and there are those in their own definition of authority who would rather that tourist honeypots did not brandish Clearances material, or even stock it. Craig writes:

> To think that such matters should and can be driven outwith the pale of ordinary discourse is to make the same mistake as the apparatchiks

Staffa from the Hollow of Dark Grazings: 'a low dark hull, not three-quarters of a mile long . . .'

*Dervaig, Mull, with its round-towered church, at dusk, a
monumental winter stillness*

who thought to exorcise all memoir of the labour camps from Soviet people's consciousness. When the Thaw came and Solzhenitsyn was allowed to publish *One Day in the Life of Ivan Denisovich*, the effect was therapeutic. One Soviet scholar called the novel a 'folk legend' with a rhythmic pattern: 'As if they were microwaves, these rhythms break up the stone which lies in our inner being and turn it to dust to be carried away by spiritual breezes, restoring like functions to the frozen parts of the soul – and in particular returning the capacity for tears and laughter.' It is the same mental freeing, and partial or ideal recompense for the old injustice, that a Muileach brings about by telling you that when the tombstone of Ulva's new proprietor, Clark, was being brought ashore, 'it could not be moved from the Ulva ferry because of the weight of the evil that was on it'.

The graffiti on the wall of Reudle schoolhouse spans a century. 'Robert MacDougall, 4th May 1894', is cut into the plaster at the top of the wall. A 'JC 1969' was not I. That was one of my stranger years. Among all the carved names are several boats and ships in varying degrees of skill, and one whale.

I sat another hour below the Hollow of the Dark Grazings and the hanging tree. The coffee steamed in my fist. The sea began to amass one more onslaught of storms to gatecrash the day's noontide lull. The blue was gone from the water, and it had begun to stripe itself gray and silver. The sky held the same shades in broader bands, a sky abstracted like Rothko paintings without the colour. In the midst of all that banding of sea and sky, and moored out in the sea's darkest, thickest band, lay Staffa.

I heard Mendelssohn in my head (who doesn't who looks on Staffa?) and I heard with a smile the refrain to his famous Fingal's Cave overture lustily bawled out during a well-lubricated ceilidh on St Kilda: 'We're going to be sea-sick, We're going to be sea-sick . . .' I have never been able to take his *Hebrides* overture seriously since then, which is a pity.

Staffa came to the world's attention in 1772 when one Joseph Banks visited it with tent and provisions for a few days. Islanders on Mull told him no one had ever been there, but he and his companion found a reclusive hird there tending a few beasts. The story goes that the hird entertained them well, fed them milk and fish, but when in the morning his guests protested that they had been assaulted by fleas, he raged at them, saying they must have brought them ashore with them!

Banks, like every visitor since, was enthralled by Staffa's volcanic fluke. What on earth was nature up to when she girdled the island cliffs in these perfectly hung pleats, hundreds of them in perfect symmetries? The Vikings had paused long enough to name the place after its colonnades of black hexagonal and pentagonal pillars of basaltic lava . . . the word means Pillar Island. Banks was told *the* cave was named after Fhinn MacCool, but long before it became world famous as Fingal's Cave, the Gaels had known of it as Uamh Binne, the Music Cave, for the ocean's repertoire of sounds in its astounding pillared, stalactited chamber. It was surely that, as much as the look of the place, which turned Mendelssohn's head that summer of 1829? Certainly there is much oceanic rhythm in the resulting overture. Some who have suffered there (including Mendelssohn himself: his companion Klingemann wrote that 'Felix . . . gets on better with the sea as an artist than his stomach does . . .') feel the room move uncertainly to the music, so unerringly has he caught the sea-sway.

It was an uncanny nine days for the twenty-year-old Mendelssohn. On July 30 he had been to Holyrood Abbey in Edinburgh, of which he wrote:

> In the twilight today we went to the Palace where Queen Mary lived
> and loved . . . the chapel beside it has now lost its roof, it is overgrown
> with grass and ivy, and at the broken altar, Mary was crowned Queen
> of Scotland. Everything is ruined, decayed and open to the sky. I believe
> I have found there today the beginning of my Scotch Symphony . . .

On 7 August he wrote a letter to his family in which he had set down that ocean-deep opening theme 'to show you how extraordinarily the Hebrides affected me'.

It is surely no coincidence that Holyrood is as famed for its colossal pillars as Staffa. Banks wrote: 'Compared to this, what are the cathedrals and palaces built by man?' I for one agree with him, but it was the man-made pillars which wrought a symphony in Mendelssohn, nature's pillars the sketch-book overture.

Staffa rears above the boats which spawn a million photographs and paintings. The impression is of a vastness of scale. From the clifftop below the Hollow of the Dark Grazings, the island is low and flat and dark and of no more account than a passing hull. There is a point on the journey back to Mull when the cliffs of Staffa have grown distant enough to lose their detail, columns and caves folded away into the depths of silhouette. It would have been good to be Joseph Banks when his boat reached that point, before he had broken the news to the unsuspecting world, that world which knew only a low, dark hull, less than 150 feet high, not three-quarters of a mile long, not half a mile wide; and the music of Uamh Binne was still unscored.

You cannot approach Iona in any frame of mind other than the pilgrim's. Nothing else works

Chapter Ten

IONA TAKES FOREVER

IONA TAKES A lot of getting to. Whether you come to proclaim Christianity and claim immortality by wicker coracle, like Columba, or more prosaically by CalMac from Oban and car through Glenmore, or corkscrewing down from Tobermory with Ben More your perpetual milestone, Iona takes forever. One of the differences between Columba and the rest of us was that he *had* forever.

You cannot approach Iona in any frame of mind other than the pilgrim's. Nothing else works. There is not enough island for tourism. There is not enough height for the mountaineer, not enough distance for the backpacker, not enough difference for the naturalist. For the pilgrim there is a four-miles-by-two portion of heaven on earth. So go as a pilgrim.

Besides, Iona's Columba-besotted past insists on it. Its present insists on its past. Those who cast an unimpressed eye on its unimpressive village and modest profile, shrug through the wind to the Abbey and huddle in the tea-room craving only the next ferry back to leafy, lofty Mull have missed the point. It is not the shape and stature of the rocks which elevate Iona above all islands – it *is* the rocks.

Iona is old. Older than most other fragments of the planet most of us are likely to step on. It was nature's foundation stone. Having laid it down, she stood on it and began to throw up other volcanoes. It is unlikely Columba knew this when he hove to in (inevitably) Columba's Bay in 563 unless his God had earmarked it for him. More likely is a traditional explanation. He had landed first on Oronsay but found he could still see the Irish coast (it must have been an uncommon day, that one). At Iona, he found he could not see it. Thus, there is a cairn near his bay called Carn Cul ri Eirrin, which translates none to silkily into the Cairn of the Back-to-Ireland. By that same tradition he buried his coracle at the beach, which suggests he missed the narrow, sheltered waters of the Sound of Iona. Tch, tch.

He could scarcely have chosen better. There was the machair for pasture, cultivatable land, a sheltered east coast, and from the high ground, outlook over as many seaward miles as any land-grabbing incomer could wish for. Wind and wet would not trouble him. He was Irish, after all. The island was also unoccupied. That fact, and a complete lack of distinguishing features from any distance were perhaps why in Gaelic it is known as I – simply 'Island'. However he chose his island destination, he began, some say wittingly, an association between Iona and the rest of the Christian world which endures unbroken nearly 1,500 years after the event. Wittingly because of a prophecy which adherents have long claimed to be his and which runs:

> In Iona of my heart, Iona of my love,
> Instead of monk's voice shall be lowing of cows
> But ere the world shall come to an end,
> Iona shall be as it was.

'A cup of tea please.'

'Are you staying or are you going on the ferry?'

'I'm going on the ferry.'

She looked out to where the boat had just begun to nose in to the pier from its offshore mooring.

'I'll better give you it in a paper cup.'

What is it about ferries, I wondered, which makes philosophers of folk?

I cupped my hand round the cup. The wind-chill factor saw to it that the hundred yards' walk reduced the tea to tepid. I sipped as I walked, tea-drinking pilgrim. It had been ten years. At the rail of the upper deck I remembered.

It had been a haphazard decision, not part of the planned stay on Mull. Ben More had been exhausting the day before, gales and stinging sleety snow had forced retreat, and this was May. Regroup the forces of endeavour behind a rock. Coffee. A dram (small one, good for the morale). Wait to see if the weather would ease. A window, a seductive blink of sun, same result. Down, cold and dismal. In the evening, May in the woods of Salen had been blissful, warm, birdsung. Iona was to be the respite day.

I remembered I had found the village a bit dismal, scruffy almost, the setting of the Abbey prosaic, the Abbey itself . . . quite wondrous. I had put churches behind me by then, finding my Gods in nature, in landscape. Iona Abbey had one extraordinary quality from within: it exuded spirituality.

Columba? Hardly. He had been dead six or seven hundred years when the Abbey was built. His had been a timber thing, modest as Iona. What then? His gift, I think, which was his granitic faith in Christian peace. Wherever else in the world that most flawed of ideals has faltered, on Iona it never has. It never has because of all who came after, pilgrims sipping sanctity or tea.

I remembered crossing the waist of the island to white sands, white as the summit snows of yesterday's Ben More. And I remembered the blue. There are all the shades of blue on earth, and then there is Iona blue. It was the first time I had been numbed by colour. It was that blue which begins at your feet where the sea lies still as a pool over white sands and flows seamlessly through deepening layers of ocean. It is blue beyond colour. That was what I remembered with the paper cup in my hand, and Rum on the starboard bow; I had forgotten about Rum on the starboard bow, and how small Staffa was.

I walked past the Abbey. I would save it for last. I wanted to climb Dun I, the lowly summit of the island. I wanted to see the white sands and I wanted to drink my fill of the Iona Blue. There was also a further purpose to my pilgrimage. It was a year to the day since my mother had died. For no reason I could lay a name to, I wanted to associate the event with the island. I am no keeper of anniversaries, especially anniversaries of deaths. I remember lives best, and need no dates to celebrate the lives of both my parents. But I was on Mull again and, given the date, I decided to make the association whatever way Iona chose to make it for me. I had thought, of course, of a quiet moment in the Abbey. Columba's gift to me was quite different.

I climbed Dun I, bullied uphill by a frantic February easterly. I crossed the summit and sat in the lee of west-facing rock. I could see white sand. I could see Iona Blue. I could see down the broad spine of the island. I could see up the ocean to Rum, and beyond it, identified by its far glimmer of high snow, the Skye Cuillin. I waved to it, because that is how I greet friends-in-landscape.

I descended to the shore where the wind filled my eyes and my hair with white sand and the Iona Blue was a song beyond music. I climbed back over the Dun I. On the summit I walked into a wall of wind which took my breath away and rammed gallons of its own icy breath down my throat. I sat. I sat because standing was too difficult. And sitting, in that rage of winds, sand-smitten and colour-drenched, I found the calm which permitted my remembrance.

I walked back to the boat without visiting the Abbey. I had made my pilgrimage. Columba, presiding spirit of pilgrims, or whatever, gave me the

'I remembered crossing the waist of the island to white sands . . .
and I remembered the Iona Blue . . .'

most vivid remembrance he could by placing it not within the confines of a building but out in the un-limitations of nature. The Abbey is merely the built focal point of what Columba's legacy has become. It is the island which is the cathedral of the pilgrim.

Back in Tobermory.
    'Did you get to Iona, then?'
    'Yes, I did.'
    'What was it like?'
    'It was freezing,' I said.

I have found this, its source unknown to me:

> Part of the inheritance of the Celt is the sense of the longing and striving after the unattainable and incomprehensible on Earth . . . Forlorn, he has the sense of fighting a losing battle for all his soul holds dear; for the simple life of old, for the beauty of the world threatened with utilitarian desecration, for outlived ideals . . .

156

*Columba could not have chosen better – machair for pasture,
cultivatable land, a sheltered east coast, and from the high ground,
outlook over many a seaward and landward mile*

*North shore, Iona: 'it is the island which is the cathedral of the
pilgrim'*

That part of me which is Celt suffers that part of the inheritance. But it must take the credit for the eye which homes in on the Iona Blue too, and the susceptibility to summit winds.

I will say this for Iona. I believe I could walk its low-slung landscape forever and not tire of its simplicities and its enduring elements. The world is not yet at an end and Iona *is* as it was. St Columba and I have one thing in common. We both know that I, the Island, Iona takes forever.

BIBLIOGRAPHY

Brown, George Mackay, *Magnus* (Hogarth, 1973)
    Fishermen with Ploughs (Hogarth, 1971)
Campbell, Marion, *Argyll* (Turnstone, 1977)
Cooper, Derek, *Hebridean Connection* (Routledge and Kegan Paul, 1977)
Craig, David, *On the Crofters' Trail* (Cape, 1990)
Crumley, Jim, *Among Mountains* (Mainstream, 1993)
    with Baxter, Colin, *St Kilda* (Baxter, 1988)
    Shetland (Baxter, 1992)
Gordon, Seton, *Afoot in Wild Places* (Cassell, 1937)
Hannah, Ian C., *The Story of Scotland in Stone* (Strong Oak, 1988)
McNeill, F. Marian, *Iona – A History of the Island* (Blackie, 1920)
Macnab, P. A., *Highways and Byways of Mull* (pub. the author, 1978)